PREACHING FOR
THESE PEOPLE

MOWBRAY PREACHING SERIES

PREACHING FOR THESE PEOPLE

ANDREW R. C. MCLELLAN

MOWBRAY

Mowbray
A Cassell imprint
Wellington House, 125 Strand, London WC2R 0BB
PO Box 605, Herndon VA 20172

First published 1997

British Library Cataloguing-in-Publication Data
A catalogue record for this book is available from the British Library.

ISBN 0-264-67432-4

The verse from the hymn by John Bell on p. 41 is © Wild Goose Resource
group, Iona Community, Glasgow G51 3UU, and reproduced by permission.
The poem by John Bell on pp. 26-8 and the verse from the hymn by Kathy
Galloway on p. 12 are reproduced by permission of the authors.

Typeset by Keystroke, Jacaranda Lodge
Printed and bound in Great Britain by Biddles Ltd, Guildford and King's Lynn

CONTENTS

In happy memory
of my father

A. B. McLellan

PREFACE

All but two of these sermons were preached in St Andrew's and St George's Church in the centre of Edinburgh. Inevitably they reflect the particular interests and style of that congregation. Like most congregations in the centre of cities, it is made up of people who travel in to it, and tends to attract people who share the values and hopes and theology of those who are already part of it. In one sense this is a real weakness, for the ideal Christian congregation would contain a complete cross-section of backgrounds and views and experience. In another sense, however, it does mean that those who listen to sermons in St Andrew's and St George's know that the type of sermon which they will hear Sunday by Sunday is likely to be addressed to them and to people like them.

So these sermons are preached for a congregation which has an open, generous, questioning understanding of Christian faith. When the members of the congregation set out their statement of purpose they included the aim 'to seek a courageous, open attitude to theological questions within the central convictions of the Christian faith'. There will always be worshippers who are not sure whether or not they would want to describe themselves as Christians. St Andrew's and St George's and its sermons continually keep in mind their responsibilities towards enquirers and seekers, and acknowledge that in so doing we are very often addressing ourselves.

Several of the sermons here are particularly addressed to two dominant interests of the congregation. Every year the Edinburgh International Festival provides a unique opportunity for Christians to reflect on issues which relate Christian faith to the arts: and every year this congregation tries to take advantage of these opportunities. Every year Christian Aid Week confronts the church with the needs of the world's poor: and again St Andrew's and St George's has tried hard to respond to these needs. There are sermons here which grow directly out of these concerns.

During the period in which these sermons were preached I was the Convener of the Church and Nation Committee of the General Assembly of the Church of Scotland. This committee has a particular responsibility for social and political questions and from time to time gave me the opportunity to visit different places in connection with its concerns. Some of these visits resulted in sermons for St Andrew's and St George's, which are represented here together with others which reflect a Christian engagement with public affairs.

ACKNOWLEDGEMENTS

This book has been shaped by the sparkle, affection and prayers of one congregation: I hope they know how much I appreciate them. John Bell gave me a meditation and Fred Booth gave me a story: for both of which I am very grateful. I am glad that there are references in these pages to the books of Frederick Buechner, Alan Paton and Margaret Hebblethwaite, for I owe a considerable debt to each of them. Ruth McCurry and Gillian Paterson have been models of courtesy and helpfulness as publishers. Most of all, my wife Irene and our sons Andi and Ian have offered fun and encouragement and light throughout the production of this book.

Part 1

Preaching about God

IS GOD A COMPUTER VIRUS?

The Magi
MATTHEW 2.1–12

Richard Dawkins is one of Britain's outstanding scientists. He is a Cambridge biologist whose brilliant book *The Selfish Gene* is a must for anyone who seeks to understand Darwinism and its relationship to religion. He is a humane, confident, highly educated and assertive atheist who enjoys taking up the cudgels against Christian faith, and recently he was at it again. He announced a theory with the question 'Is God a computer virus?', and it is too important for us to run away from.

Dawkins' argument comes from his vast knowledge of cellular biology and his reasonable understanding of computers. He argues that the human mind is peculiarly prone to viruses because, like DNA cells and like computers, it is ready to reproduce information accurately, and it is ready to obey instructions encoded in the information it receives. This part of his argument is fairly technical, but I think you will be interested in the symptoms he suggests would mark the sufferer of a virus of the mind.

If religion is a virus of the mind, then Dawkins suggests that the patient would be driven by some deep inner conviction that something is true, a conviction which seems to owe nothing to evidence or reason. Tell the truth, is he not right that religion sometimes does appear in that form?

Another symptom would be the conviction that mystery itself is a good thing and that it is a bad thing to solve mysteries. He writes: 'It is as though the faithful gain prestige through managing to believe even more ridiculous things than their rivals succeed in believing . . . Any wimp in

2

religion could believe that bread symbolically represents the body of Christ, but it takes a real red-blooded Catholic to believe something as daft as transubstantiation.' Is he not right, that sometimes religion, Protestantism as much as Catholicism, revels in obscurity?

A third symptom of religious virus suggested by Dawkins is the ease with which it is caught from those round about: what he calls 'epidemiology'. It is statistically overwhelmingly likely, he argues, that people who have a faith will find it is the same faith as their parents and grandparents had. 'The convictions that you so passionately believe would have been a completely different, and largely contradictory set of convictions if you happened to be born in a different place.' Accidents of birth rather than evidence. Is he not right?

Where would you begin to respond? With the argument about inner convictions compelling believers in the absence of any evidence? First of all, that is not true. The exhaustive and scientific study of the Bible is evidence. What the first Christians felt about Jesus is evidence. The story of the church's life is evidence. The experience of people known to you is evidence. Your own experience is evidence. Second, religion is not unique in finding its source in inner convictions as well as evidence. Van Gogh painting, a mother duck teaching the little ones to swim, a son making arrangements for his father's funeral, even Crick and Watson, Dawkins' great predecessors in chasing the discovery of the DNA molecule: if religion is driven by inner convictions to go beyond the available evidence then it is in company with some of the finest and most creative and most noble instincts in the world.

Second, there is the symptom of mystery as an end in itself: the odder the claim, the more likely religious people are to believe it. Again, I make two responses. First, it is not true. Anyone who has taken part in a study group at St Andrew's and St George's will know how reluctant Scottish Presbyterians are to take anything on trust. Scepticism and faith are often close neighbours. Second, Dawkins is wrong to give mystery a bad name. Deliberate muddle is no good;

but mystery is an important part of life. Ask young lovers; ask anyone in the Cathedral of Chartres; ask scientists themselves: the matchless physicist Richard Feynman used to begin his lectures on quantum mechanics thus: 'I think I can safely say that nobody understands quantum mechanics.'

Dawkins' third symptom of the virus of religion was that you caught it from your friends and family rather than by weighing up the issues. As a parent, I sometimes wish that were more true: if faith is a virus it sometimes appears singularly unwilling to take up house with those it contacts. At its best, it is a weak argument. What he detects as infection is really to do with opportunity. For every opportunity there is for a child in a Scottish manse to assess the value of Islam, there are a thousand opportunities to respond to Christianity. Indeed, it would be extraordinary if religion appeared quite haphazardly all over the earth: if the normal affair was a Buddhist, a Christian and a Sikh all living in the same family. People making choices about eternity and the meaning of life without any reference to those they love and trust would certainly seem to me a much more irrational, haphazard and random business. What you do find is exactly what I would expect to find if normal people cared about sharing precious things with those they love.

On this Sunday the gospel story set for us is Matthew's story of magi coming to bow before the infant Jesus. These people were early scientists: experts in the learning of their day. There is a profound symbolism in these scientists bringing their gifts and kneeling before Christ. The world of science today is far too important to be left on its own.

Science wrestles heroically with the deepest questions about the meaning of life – is not that what science is really about? – think of those people coming to Bethlehem to kneel before him who was with God from the beginning, without whom was not anything made that was made. Science opens up the mysteries and the questions at the very centre of things: think of those wise men coming to Bethlehem and kneeling before him who is the Alpha and the Omega, the beginning and the end. Science is about

4

change – understanding in order to change – think of those wise men coming to Bethlehem to kneel before him who is the power of God and the wisdom of God. Christians need not, Christians, even non-scientific Christians, must not, be afraid of science.

We read also this morning from the letter to the Romans: 'Those who have never been told of him shall see, and those who have never heard of him shall understand.' Our task is to listen, to understand, and to trust that the Lord of Life is the Lord of science too.

And this footnote. Just when I thought I had this sermon neatly tied up and I was feeling quite pleased with it – this sermon on 'Is God a computer virus?' – for the first time since I started to use the machine, the computer on which I prepare all my sermons refused to operate! Was it providence, or just a queer coincidence – could Richard Dawkins be right after all? Amen.

WHAT LETTER WOULD YOU CHOOSE?

I am the Alpha and the Omega.
REVELATION 1.8

In the touching autobiography of an American writer there was this moment by the bedside of his dying-mother-in-law. He writes: 'She was not only a great lady, which is one thing, but also a good woman, which is another . . . The last time I can remember perching on the side of her bed myself, I asked her an utterly absurd question which happened to occur to me. If she could be any letter of the alphabet she wanted to be, I said, which letter would she choose? The answer she gave me was so faint that I had to bend down to hear. It was the letter Z. She wanted to stick around as long as she could possibly stick it.'

An utterly absurd question, of course. If you could be any letter of the alphabet, what would you choose? Ask God that question, and the answer is 'I am the Alpha and the Omega'. Apparently God is a Greek speaker; so could not have chosen Z anyway; but might, I suppose, have chosen, for example, π. Which is the ratio between the diameter and the circumference of a circle: π stands for the number 3.1416. A bit silly as a symbol for God, you might say, unless you knew that π is technically known as a transcendental number. I only discovered that this week and I thought it might have real possibilities for a sermon, since I knew that *transcendental* meant *supernatural*, or *mystical*. Maybe π might be just the very letter for God, I thought: until I read the next line and discovered that *transcendental* also means for mathematicians 'a number which cannot be the root of any algebraic equation

6

with rational coefficients'. Not quite what I'm looking for in a letter for God after all!

But another letter from the Greek alphabet also used in mathematics is more promising. Σ is a sign in mathematics which means *the sum*, everything added together. So if you write Σ 4 to 8 you mean all the numbers between four and eight added together. Everything joined in the whole. Now that makes sense for a letter for God. The Bible has a good deal of material about God as completeness, as filling everything, as the one in whom all things come together. The language of prayer has the same: 'God, who art in all and for all and through all.' The geologist Teilhard de Chardin wrote 'In the life which wells up in me, in the matter which sustains me I find much more than God's gifts. It is God himself whom I find, the one who makes me participate in being, who moulds me.' Σ, the sum, everything added together; that might have been quite an appropriate letter for God to choose.

I'm certain that the letter which God nearly chose, however, from the Greek alphabet was not π nor Σ but T. It is the letter T, but it has had a life of its own, especially in the world of art. For T has always looked like a cross. And if you were to ask which letter God would most want to be, there is a very good case for T.

'There was a cross in the heart of God from the beginning', said the old teacher: certainly no intelligent reader of the New Testament can form the heretical view that the cross was an emergency plan by which God tried to rescue what had gone horribly wrong. Rather the cross, Jesus Christ crucified, is what God has always been, is now, and ever shall be. What we know of God is what we know in the cross; the God whom we know is the God who meets us in the cross. It is no accident that the universal Christian symbol is a cross.

Were you there when they crucified my Lord?
Were you there when they crucified my Lord?
O, sometimes it causes me to tremble, tremble, tremble.
Were you there when they crucified my Lord?

I think that if I had been writing the book of Revelation I might well have had God say 'My letter is T'. The letter of the Cross.

But I did not write the book of Revelation. So the Word of God for us this morning is 'I am the Alpha and the Omega'. These are the two letters that God chooses, out of all the letters, to have the chance to be. A and Ω. I'm pretty sure that God knows the Bible: but these two letters persuade me that John the Divine, who wrote Revelation, knew the Bible too. For there's no doubt this verse remembers Isaiah: 'Thus says the Lord, I am the first and I am the last; and there is no God but me.' Maybe the idea there is not so very far from the idea of Σ and the sum of everything. Isaiah and Revelation want us to come to God in all God's totality and completeness and continuity. Alpha and Omega. The first and the last. It's almost a proverb. 'She knows Renaissance painting from A to Z.' Indeed, the old rabbis had the very same proverb: they used to say, in the Greek translation, Abraham kept the law of God from Alpha to Omega. No wonder the letters God chooses to be are these letters. The first and the last. Nowhere where God is not already. No time when God is not already. Nowhere where God will not be. No time where God will not be. All, all, all belongs to God and beyond God's care and power and love there is no possibility of going.

God chooses to be Alpha. This is about beginnings, about origins. This title for God does invite you to speculate about cosmology, about the universe and its beginnings, about a brief history of time, about the Hubble telescope. It invites you to speculate about the recent startling conclusion of the world's leading astronomers that the universe is six billion years old and that the oldest stars in it are ten billion years old. I cannot begin to understand what that means, but I try to use it at least as a measure of humility and smallness, and a measure of wonder and greatness. I and all of us and the whole human race are very tiny players in God's universe; and it is good and healthy and Christian to remember that. Yet I and you and the whole human race are especially

8

precious to the holy, hidden being who is Alpha, who holds the stars in place, who is Creator, from whose energy and love all being comes.

God chooses to be Omega. This is about ends, about conclusion and purpose. About the movement of all creation. Modern thinking about purpose and movement in creation tends to get imprisoned either in philosophical debates about progress, which may really be a trap, or in scientific debates about environmental catastrophe, which is a vital question for us all. But theological thinking, Christian thinking about end, about purpose, about conclusion, is also thinking about God. About the God who chooses the letter Ω. About God whose creation and whose will and whose purpose is to bring all children to glory; about God who works and loves and waits; about God who will be God for ever and ever.

I am Alpha and Omega. God chooses letters about beginnings and endings; about origins and purpose. But even that, colossal though it is, is not enough. For that verse, these letters, might be the word of God particularly for you. This is not just the story of God; this is your story. The classic commentary on Revelation explains that God as Alpha and Omega is 'the one in whom Christians are perpetually confronted with the Beginning and the End'. Perpetually confronted. Always for you, God is your beginning and your ending. Always, for you, God is the one whose will and purpose and love are the very source of your own life, who gave you breath and being and body and soul. God is the one whose dream you are. And always, for you, God is the one who longs to draw you to attract you, to gather you, to be there for you, to bring you home. Always. In the moment of your birth, in all the moments of your living, in the moment of your dying. 'I am Alpha and Omega, says the Lord God, who was and who is and who is to come.'

T. S. Eliot's poem *East Coker* begins 'In my beginning is my end' and it ends 'In my end is my beginning'.

FACES OF GOD

*Does not wisdom call? . . . 'Ages ago I was set up, at the first,
before the beginning of the earth . . . when he established the
heavens I was there.'*
PROVERBS 8.1, 23

In that unique passage which we read from the book of
Proverbs, it is not quite accurate to say that the figure of
Wisdom equals God. But it is accurate to say that the figure
of Wisdom is used to help to say some things about God.
This morning let's be helped by Proverbs chapter 8 to see
four faces of God.

First, the Wisdom of God is feminine in gender. She 'lifts
her voice . . . she takes her stand at the crossroads'. God is
neither male nor female. Speaking about God as masculine
is appropriate and biblical; so is speaking about God as
feminine. To say that God is like a father does not mean that
he needs to shave every day; to say that God is like a mother
is not saying anything anatomical.

I know that some people are upset when I speak in this
way. I want to reassure you that there is no real reason for
anxiety in what I am saying. The points about feminine
language about God are three. First, the theological one
I have just made: God is not male and not female. Second,
the biblical point I have just made: the language of the
Bible does allow us to use female symbols about God. Third,
a point about our own nourishment. If we allow exclusive
use of male language to create for ourselves an exclusively
male image of God, then we miss so much that is good for
us.

I want you to be clear about this. I am not against male
language about God. But I am against the exclusion of
female language in the name of theology and of the Bible

and of our own nourishment. It was six hundred years ago that the English mystic, Julian of Norwich, said: 'As truly as God is our Father, so truly also God is our Mother . . . Beautiful and sweet is our heavenly Mother in the sight of our souls; and in the sight of our heavenly Mother, dear and lovely are the gracious children.'

The second face of God in this passage about Wisdom is a face of fun. Listen to the words again: 'Then I was at his side each day, his darling and delight, playing in his presence continually, playing over his whole world, while my delight was in the human race.'

When I came back from holiday I mentioned that on successive days we had been to the battlefield of the Somme and a fun-park called Bagatelle. And I said that there is a kind of trivial Christianity which goes every day to Bagatelle but never goes to the Somme. On the other hand there is a kind of morbid Christianity which goes every day to the Somme and never goes to Bagatelle. If there is any truth in the popular image of the guilt-ridden duty-bound soul of the Scottish Christian, then sometimes we need to go to the fun-park. We need to let God take us to the fun-park. We need to remember Proverbs and the Wisdom of God 'playing continually . . . playing over his whole world'.

An American novelist and preacher called Frederick Buechner remembered the moment that changed life for him. He was an aimless student in New York when he drifted into a church and heard the great George Buttrick preaching. It was a sermon on the kingship of Jesus, crowned again and again in the hearts of the people who believe in him. And that inward coronation takes place, Buttrick said, 'among confession, and tears, and great laughter'. It was the phrase 'great laughter' that did it for Buechner. Take it home with you. Jesus is crowned 'among confession and tears and great laughter'.

A feminine face of God. A fun face of God. Now, a creative face of God. Wisdom sings: 'When there were no depths I was brought forth . . . When he established the heavens I was there . . . when he marked out the foundations

11

of the earth, then I was beside him, like a master worker; and I was daily his delight.'

Creating is what God is always doing, making things new, making things lovely. As we sang earlier in that hymn about the Spirit of God,

> She comes with artist's joyfulness
> To make and shape and sing
> She gives her hands and from them grows
> A free and lovely thing. (K. Galloway)

Rebuilding lives after disaster. Picking up the pieces after disappointment. Opening doors after failure. These are some of the ways God's creative face is shown to us. Here is another. Every October we ask all our members to consider their givings to the church. But we should also give thanks for what our money is able to do. The money we give to central church funds cares for the mentally handicapped, supports missionary partners, trains probationer ministers, pays salaries in struggling congregations and works with prostitutes. All that is God's creativity.

The fourth face of God from chapter 8 of Proverbs is the Christlike face. Feminine and fun, creative and Christlike. Do you remember that I said that this passage of Proverbs had been vastly important for the writing of the New Testament? I was thinking of the opening of St John's gospel, 'In the beginning was the Word', where the roots of that pre-existent independent being with God from the beginning are indisputably to be found in Proverbs chapter 8. And I was thinking of passages from St Paul like the one we read this morning: 'Christ crucified . . . the power of God and the wisdom of God . . . he became for us wisdom from God.' In that and similar passages St Paul does not simply mean that Christ shows us how to be clever. He means that all the Bible spoke of in the Wisdom passages of the Old Testament, all the faces of God that Wisdom shows, these are become real and alive and human and for us in Jesus Christ of Nazareth.

I know that is very difficult. But it is the centre of the gospel. All the faces of God are Christlike faces. When God comes to meet us in this communion service he comes to us as he has come to the world in Jesus Christ. Whatever you have seen of truth or beauty or compassion or forgiveness or love or healing in Jesus Christ, that is who God is for you in this communion. A book called *The Christlike God* begins with a terrific quotation from Michael Ramsey, a former Archbishop of Canterbury. Use it for your meditation during the serving of communion. 'God is Christlike, and in him is no unChristlikeness at all.' Amen.

IN THE HEART OF GOD

Herod and Pontius Pilate gathered together . . . to do whatever your
hand and your plan had predestined to take place.
ACTS 4.27, 28

Providence. A text about Providence. Where in God is
Providence to be found? Not, I think, in God's eyes. God
does not see the future. God does not see the future in the
sense of one who is able to peer ahead and know what is
going to happen. The film *Groundhog Day* is about a man
who lives the same day over and over again. At first it is great
fun: he can drive dangerously, rob banks, seduce girls – no
retribution will follow, because next day the whole thing
begins again. He always knows what is going to happen,
because yesterday he was there before. And it ends up as
hell; he despairs of being able to get out of these yesterdays
and tries suicide, and suicide, and suicide. In the end –
I won't tell you how – the spell is broken. The spell of being
compelled to relive the past is broken. He is released
from the nightmare of omniscience into the freshness and
vulnerability of a genuinely new day – a tomorrow that isn't
yesterday. He walks in new snow.

I think that is a parable for God as well. If God were to
know the future in that sense, then there would be no future:
for what makes future is that it is unknown, unformed, risky,
it hasn't happened before. And it is that for God as well.
Unknown, risky. The future is not a pretend unknown, but
a real unknown. If you think that is true for God – and I
must be honest and say that most orthodox theology thinks
that somehow it is different for God – it might be true for
God that the future for him too is genuinely future,
unknown and risky, then you might be stumbling into one of

14

the most important movements in modern theology. They call it 'process theology'. The great names in it are Alfred North Whitehead and Charles Hartshorne; and the central conviction of process theology is that God is himself somehow growing and changing. If so, then perhaps it makes sense to say that God cannot see the future; for the future only happens when it becomes present to God as well as to us.

Providence is not in God's eyes. Nor is Providence in God's hands. God cannot push the world around. Here again I am aware that what I am saying has not always been seen as orthodox theology. Indeed, the great master John Calvin specifically taught that God does push the world around: 'It is certain that not a drop of rain falls without the express command of God.' But I don't believe that. I don't believe that God makes everything happen that does happen. And I don't believe in the kind of God who controls and compels all that goes on in the world – what they call an 'interventionist God' – for two reasons.

First, the kind of God who is supposed to make everything happen that does happen looks pretty near to a monster. A few years ago there was a televised debate in this church about AIDS. It was early days and passion ran high. One minister proclaimed that AIDS was the punishment of God on a sexually wayward generation. Immediately my old teacher and my friend Murdo Ewen Macdonald jumped to his feet shaking with anger and denounced this wicked theology. 'How can you worship a god who strikes down unlettered people in Haiti, victims of drug pushers in Manhattan, children, children in Edinburgh just to prove he is a moral god and ought to be listened to? I would not treat my own children in that way and I will not believe in a god who is worse than I am.' *Days of Grace* is a memoir of the last years of Arthur Ashe, the tennis star who died of AIDS after receiving infected blood. He writes in it in a wonderfully mature way of Providence: 'I do not waste time pleading with God to make me well. I was brought up to believe that prayer is not to be invoked to ask God for things for oneself. Rather prayer is a medium through which I ask God to show me God's will and to give me strength to carry out that will.'

Second, if God's hands push everything around in the world then human beings are reduced to mere puppets, to toy soldiers in the hands of the celestial games-player. I know that is not how it is. I know that is not how it is because the fierce and painful and exhilarating business of living my own life simply does not feel at all like that. It is a grotesque perversion of the seriousness of life, of the achievements of art and the pain and joy of love and the opportunity of work to reduce it to the predetermined consequences of divine script-writing. What's more, I don't believe for a moment that Jesus held that view. If anything is clear above all from the teaching of Jesus it is the importance of our moral choices, the necessity for us to seek and work for what is right. I can't believe that God has it all wrapped up in a sealed envelope somewhere.

Providence is not in God's eyes. He doesn't see the future all written out. Providence is not in God's hands: he does not simply make everything happen. So where to look for Providence? That remains a key question if we are to be faithful to the Bible. For the Bible is full of the words that will not go away. Joseph says to his brothers 'You meant to do me harm, but God meant to bring good out of it'. Jesus said that God 'causes the sun to rise on good and bad alike, and sends the rain on the innocent and the wicked'. And Peter and John proclaim Providence when they prayed to God 'Herod and Pontius Pilate conspired . . . to do all the things which under your hand and by your decree were fore-ordained'.

Not in God's eyes, not in God's hands. Seek Providence in God's heart. It is in God's heart that Providence is to be met. For Providence is about the will of God, about his purposes, about what he will bring about. The doctrine of Providence is a statement of faith in who God is, in the kind of things he cares about. Faith in his gracious and loving purposes; faith in his determination and his capacity to bring good out of evil and to move and cherish and help the world

16

and the human race and you towards his kingdom where 'all we have willed or hoped or dreamed of good shall exist'.

There is an old Chinese story which is not Christian but which is a help. It is the story of the Old Man at the Fort. An old man was living with his son at an abandoned fort at the top of a hill. One day he lost his horse, and the neighbours came to express their sympathy. But the old man asked 'How do you know this is bad luck?' A few days afterwards his son returned with a number of wild horses! So his neighbours came again, this time to congratulate him. But the old man replied 'How do you know this is good luck?' With so many horses around his son took to riding, and it wasn't long before there was a broken leg in the family! Once more the neighbours came around to express their sympathy. But the old man was not to be moved. He answered 'How do you know this is bad luck?' The next year there was a war, and because the old man's son was lame he didn't have to go to the front!

You don't have to be Chinese to get the point. You don't have to be a Christian to get the point. But you do have to be a Christian to go farther, to say the last word. For the point about Providence is not just about our partial knowledge. It is also about God and his loving will, and his determination that, among many second-last words, he will have the last word. Last week my wife received a letter which had these words: 'More and more I believe that if God does not bring his hurt and defeated children to some final triumph, then all is lost.' Or, as St Paul said, 'If Christ is not raised, we are most miserable'. But if we were to risk the faith that Christ is raised, then the Providence of God is ours: not a magic crystal-gazing, not a heavenly manipulation, but a faithful, gracious, loving and unconquerable purpose for us all. Amen.

17

EVERYONE SHOULD BE SAVED

God desires everyone to be saved.
1 TIMOTHY 2.4

In the textbook everybody uses for 1 Timothy I looked up our text – 'God . . . desires everyone to be saved' – not much wrong with that, you would say – and I read this: 'All down Christian history this sentence has provoked intense heart-searching and controversy.' 'God's will is that everyone should be saved' . . . 'intense heart-searching and controversy'? For goodness sake! Is this man talking sense?

Yes he is. This seemingly harmless, almost sentimental thought is one of the real problems of the New Testament. How can the Bible speak here about salvation for everyone and speak in other places about salvation only for those whom he chooses in Christ? The Bible clearly speaks about the judgement of God and about everlasting fire. Is it God's will that all should be saved?

There are four ways you can deal with this text. It says that God's will is that everyone should be saved. The first way to deal with that is to say that the text does not mean what it says. All sorts of heavy-weight scholars, including the massive St Augustine, argue that 'all' does not really mean 'all'. What is really meant is that God's will is that all 'whom he has already chosen' should be saved. Or, to put it another way, that God's will is that all who should be saved should be saved. Well, St Augustine was better at it than I am; and no doubt there are some here who are pleased with that solution; but to me it sounds artificial and over-subtle and – dare I say it? – a bit of a cheat.

The second way you can deal with this text is to say

that it is right. The salvation of all is what God wills, and what God wills he does. The technical name for this kind of thinking is 'universalism', and I hope you like it for at least two reasons. One is that I hope you have a natural instinct to take the Bible seriously: and if the Bible says that God wills the salvation of all and not merely some, then you are predisposed to believe it until persuaded otherwise. The second reason I hope you might be persuaded that the text is true is because of what you believe of the love of God. If God is love, and if he loves bad people, and if his will will be done, then how can it be that he would see any creature he has made perish or be destroyed or go to hell? Surely above all the conviction about God that Christians would want to hold on to and defend is his universal love? Does that not mean that somehow all will be saved?

I wish it was as simple as that. I want that to be true; and I will be very surprised if you do not want that to be true. But in fact nearly all Christians at nearly all times have believed that to be not true. Recently I did a 'Thought for the Day' on radio: it was about the death of a friend of mine who had worked for the BBC. It ended with the words 'what God has done in raising Jesus from death he will do with those whom we have loved'. Jane Franchi had hardly said 'thank you' before a minister was rebuking me for saying that. It sounded like universalism, he told me, and that must be stopped. In 1846 the Professor of Theology at King's College London, F. D. Maurice, was sacked from his job because they suspected him of universalism.

Why should the belief that God's will is to save everyone be rejected by nearly all Christians at nearly all times? One reason is that Jesus seems to tell stories, like the one we read this morning, which imply that God will reject some. Another reason is that the judgement of God is real and critical and not to be brushed aside. The horrors of Bosnia and the sexual abuse of children and what nuclear weapons have done to the human soul really matter; most universalists don't take evil with nearly enough seriousness. Perhaps the most powerful argument against universalism is to do with human free will. If we are really free, and not simply puppets in God's puppet play, then we must be free to say 'no' to God; and that must be a real choice with real meaning, and not just a 'pretend'. If you want to say that 1 Timothy 2.4 is right, then you have a terrific amount of thinking to do.

Our text is that 'God desires everyone to be saved'. The third approach to the text is to say that it is wrong. I certainly hope that you would have the courage to say that about many verses in the Bible: one of the signs of grown-up Christianity is that it thinks about what the Bible says rather than merely agreeing with everything in it. What is more, I hope you would tend to feel that the whole weight of Christian tradition – and the whole weight of Christian tradition is against universalism – is to be listened to. Plenty of the Christians who have gone before us were neither fools nor knaves.

But it is not as simple as that on this side either. For if you want to hold to the conviction that there is an alternative fate as well as eternal peace and joy – call it rejection or damnation or punishment or annihilation or hell or whatever you like – then you have some very hard things to face as well. There is the question of the limit of God's power. It is a weird kind of trust in God and a weird kind of proclamation of his sovereignty which argues that in the end of the day the power of sin and evil to destroy, or the power of the individual to say 'no', are stronger than the power of God to heal and restore. Then there is the question of Jesus and his death on the cross. That must be for Christians the centre of their thinking about these issues. Surely the whole point of the death of Jesus is the openness, the arms stretched out, the rejection of none?

Let me go farther. It is a grotesque idea of God which suggests that he and those whom he chooses could enjoy eternal bliss and joy and peace while aware that others scream in the tortures of the damned. Such a vision is contemptible: what would we think of a human being who satisfied his thirst for revenge so implacably? Is it not the case that the most murderous tendencies in the history of the

20

Christian church have been fuelled by the conviction that since unbelievers, Jews, heathens, natives – call them what you will – are going to hell anyway they do not matter? Defending the doctrine that the damnation or the rejection of some is God's will is terribly difficult: at least as difficult as the opposite.

So the fourth approach to our text is to say we do not know. Shakespeare called death 'the undiscover'd country from whose bourn no traveller returns'. Who can know what lies beyond death? Who can reconcile the contradictory forces in the traditions of Christian theology? Who can wrestle with the logical conundrums of human freedom and divine love? Who can see into the heart of God?

Who can see into the heart of God? Well, I dare to say that I can. Through a glass, darkly; but not seeing nothing. For I have seen Jesus of Nazareth and heard the story of his cross. And I believe that there is nothing in God, nothing at all in God, which can be different from Jesus and his cross. So whatever God is like, and whatever his rules for judging the world – what the Westminster Confession calls his 'eternal decrees' – I am certain that there cannot be dark sides, unknown sides, secrets in God which are not compatible with the infinite, painful, personal, sacrificial love that is shown and given and shared and poured out for us in the life of Jesus. Anything less than that, any God who is merely logic or merely theology or merely Bible texts or merely how we believe a parent should act – anything less than the God and Father of our Lord Jesus Christ – I will have none of it.

Many a sermon on this theme ends with a verse by the American poet Whittier:

I know not where his islands lift
Their fronded palms to air
I only know I cannot drift
Beyond his love and care.

But this sermon is going to end with the forty-eighth paraphrase: St Paul at his most Christian:

21

Nor death nor life nor earth nor hell
Nor time's destroying sway
Can e'er efface us from his heart
Or make his love decay.
Each future period that will bless
As it has blessed the past.
He loved us from the first of time
He loves us to the last. Amen.

WHAT IS HEAVEN LIKE?

What no eye has seen, nor ear heard, nor the human heart
conceived, what God has prepared for those who love him – these
things God has revealed to us through the Spirit.
1 CORINTHIANS 2.9

When the former minister of this congregation died last week, a life of 92 years came to a close. A life of 92 years, 66 of them as a minister of the Church of Scotland, many of them as minister of this congregation. And there are people here today, and many more in the communion of saints already, who have good cause to be grateful to God for that life. He was old, he was frail, he was alone, he was ready to die. What must heaven be like for him?

When John died, my son was standing beside him. Perhaps you read about the schoolboy who collapsed recently watching a rugby match and was dead before he hit the ground. He was chatting to Ian when he died. John was seventeen, extremely popular, the least cruel of youngsters, and super-fit. Of course his death raises all sorts of theological questions, and I can assure you we've been living some of them; but the particular theological question which interests me this morning is what must heaven be like for a dynamic, virile, energetic seventeen-year-old?

How can heaven be heaven for an old minister and a seventeen-year-old boy at the same time? At first thought it is either going to be a little exhausting for the one or a little dull for the other! One of the earliest pictures of heaven, and one of the best loved, raises that very problem. This is Isaiah:

The wolf shall live with the lamb, the leopard shall lie down with the kid, the calf and the lion and the fatling together, and a little child shall lead them. The cow and the bear shall graze, their young shall lie down together; and the lion shall eat straw like the ox. The nursing child shall play over the hole of the asp, and the weaned child shall put its hand on the adder's den. They will not hurt or destroy on all my holy mountain; for the earth will be full of the knowledge of the Lord as the waters cover the sea.

Which is all very well: but it won't quite do: for it expects the lion to stop being a lion and to become a big cuddly calf; it expects the asp to stop being a snake and become a legless kitten. Whereas pure Christian theology and real orthodox faith is looking for a way of talking about heaven which allows the lion to become a perfect lion, allows the asp to become a perfect asp; allows our former minister to be glorified as himself, and allows John to be resurrected as John. That is the meaning of the statement in the Apostles' Creed 'I believe in the resurrection of the body'.

For the last few weeks we've been looking at this book, *Credo* by Hans Küng, and I cannot disagree with those who find it difficult. Nor can I disagree with those who find it superb. Today is the last chapter. The last words of the Apostles' Creed: 'I believe in the resurrection of the body and the life everlasting.' In a very wide-ranging chapter this morning we think about heaven. What is heaven like?

Küng says three simple things. Heaven is not a place. I'm interested that he stresses that, for I simply assume that very few people think of heaven in terms of geography or astronomy. But this professor suggests I am wrong. So for clarity let us say that God does not dwell 'above' the world in a physical sense: no amount of space exploration is ever going to confirm or deny what Christians believe about heaven and about God.

Second, heaven is not automatic. All credit to Hans Küng, he takes very seriously the dimension of hell in Christian thought. And he is right to do so, for to empty the judgement of God of seriousness is to trivialize God. Yet Küng strongly affirms that even talk of hell can only be done in a Christian way if you talk first and last about mercy and hope: 'The punishment of hell, like everything else, remains subordinate to God, his will and his grace.' On the one hand, those who are in danger of passing over the infinite seriousness of their personal responsibility are warned that their salvation is not automatically guaranteed. On the other hand, those who are in danger of despairing at the infinite seriousness of their personal responsibility are encouraged to believe that there are no limits to God's grace.

And the third thing that Küng says about heaven is that by definition words will not do. Heaven is beyond the experience of our words. In the play *Amadeus* the tragedy of Salieri is that he alone is able to recognize that the music of Mozart, as he says, 'is the voice of God, is given to us to show us heaven'. A child's face lit up with laughter, the bread and wine of the communion table, coming home being forgiven, St Andrews in the sunshine, the community of care that grows up around an AIDS victim – words will not do.

So who but a fool would try to use words to speak of heaven? Who but a fool, or a preacher! For I want you to believe in heaven, to love heaven, to be confident about heaven. I want that for your living and I want that for your dying. But what words will do?

There are the words of the Bible. As it happened I was in the school where the boy died last week a couple of hours after he had died and without warning the housemaster asked me to go and say something to 80 weeping boys who had lost someone they had lived with for years, my own son among them. I don't remember what I said, but I do know that the only thing any of them remembered, but many of them did remember, was that I said that there is nothing in death or life which can separate us from the love of God. I suspect hardly any of them recognized chapter 8 of Romans, but it was what they needed. At another time it might be the psalms, 23 or 121 or 103; or that terrific resurrection chapter we read a little of this morning: 1 Corinthians 15, or the visions of the book of Revelation, or almost anything from the second half of St John's gospel. Of course words won't do for heaven, and of course these words are only hints or pictures, but my goodness, they bring healing and hope.

Then there are the words which people have come to love from outside the Bible. The one which the school chaplain used last week is one which I've often used at funerals, and indeed many people here have asked me to use.

> Death is nothing at all . . . I have only slipped away into the next room. I am I and you are you. Whatever we were to each other, that we are still. Call me by the old familiar name, speak to me in the easy way which you always used . . . Life means all that it ever meant. it is the same as it ever was; there is absolutely unbroken continuity. Why should I be out of mind because I am out of sight? I am waiting for you for an interval, somewhere very near, just around the corner. All is well. (Henry Scott Holland)

Now in one sense that doesn't tell you anything about heaven. How could it? And yet so many people have found their hope, their trust, their faith in heaven strengthened by it. If that kind of writing is what you need, then the book you want is *All in the End is Harvest*, an anthology for those who grieve: a book which has in it nearly all the famous bits, prose and poetry, and some lovely prayers as well.

What is heaven? Words won't do. Yet I persist with one more attempt. Six or seven years ago I was involved in the consequences of a horrific road accident on Queensferry Road in which five teenagers were killed. When I had to conduct some kind of memorial service in the school I felt utterly inadequate. So I turned to one of my friends and asked for help. Overnight John Bell wrote this piece which I used at the service; and I dug it out again this week because of the death of my son's friend. It is called 'I never wanted to be born':

> I never wanted to be born.

> The older I grew,
> the fonder I became

26

of my mother's womb
and its warmth and safety.

I feared the unknown:
    the next world,
about which I knew nothing
but imagined the worst.

Yet as I grew older,
I sensed in my soul
that the womb was not my home forever.

Though I did not know when,
I felt sure that one day
I would disappear through a door
which had yet to be opened,
and confront the unknown
of which I was afraid.

And then,
it happened.

In blood, tears and pain,
it happened.

I was cut off from the familiar:
I let my life behind
and discovered not darkness but light
    not hostility but love
    not eternal separation
but hands that wanted to hold me.

(*Pause*)

I never wanted to be born.

I don't want to die.

The older I grow,
the fonder I become
of this world
and its warmth
and its safety.

I fear the unknown
  the next world
about which I know nothing
but imagine the worst.

Yet as I grow older
I sense in my soul
that this world is not my home forever.

Though I do not know when,
I feel that one day
I will disappear through a door
which has yet to be opened.

Perhaps having come so safely through the first door
I should not fear so hopelessly the second.

Amen.

Part 2

Preaching about Jesus

CHOOSING A NAME

He was given the name Jesus, the name given by the
angel before he was conceived.
LUKE 2.21

You will not find a throat that did not catch with the story
of the little baby boy left for dead recently in the hospital
mortuary; until his father went to see the body for the last
time and saw him move. What made the story particularly
poignant was that the little chap's name was Jesus. Spanish
Catholics regularly call their sons Jesus; that emphasizes
the continuity between Jesus of Nazareth and ourselves, our
co-humanity, and that is an authentic Christian instinct.
Protestants, as far as I know, never call their sons Jesus; and
that emphasizes the distance between our humanity and that
of Jesus of Nazareth, the discontinuity; and that is an
authentic Christian instinct also.

When Mary and Joseph called the Bethlehem baby Jesus
they were not doing anything unusual. It is the Greek form
of the old name Joshua; and like many names from the Bible
it has a splendid meaning to the ears of faith: 'God saves';
and it was the name of one of the great heroes of their
people. It was Joshua who had brought the wanderers from
Egypt into the promised land after the death of Moses. They
went for tradition for the baby's name. Not that they had
much choice. For the scriptures go out of their way to
emphasize that this name was given to them. More than
once does the Bible make the point. Mary and Joseph were
not free to choose the name. That strikes me as peculiar.
Why on earth should it make any difference? Does your
name say anything about who you are?

30

Let's pretend they could have chosen any name they liked for the child of destiny, for the one who, the angel said, would be 'Emmanuel, God with us'. And let's pretend they were real trendies. Looking for real contemporary names for the baby. Last week I was served my sandwich in Princes Street by Kylie; and I once baptized a child called Toyah McMillan. Let's pretend that Mary is looking for a name which would say something about the times we live in and what we really need.

Then they might have called the baby Sigmund. It would be difficult to overestimate the importance of Dr Freud of Vienna for the way the whole world, or at least the world in the North and West, thinks today. No doubt today's psychiatrists rarely hold strict Freudian principles without modification, but Sigmund started a process which has changed everything. In court-room and in classroom and in television studio the importance of the insights of psycho-analysis is taken for granted.

Not for a moment do I regret that. I have known people whose lives were transformed and liberated by brilliant treatment from Freudian practitioners. My most enduring memory from my years as chaplain in Scotland's prison for women was the repeated confirmation of the truth of Freud's primary insight: that the very early experience of children, especially in sexual matters, can mark and cripple them for life. No Christian minister who has baptized a baby or who has read the nativity stories in the gospels is likely to disparage the Freudian thesis that 'the child is in the midst'. But as a system for society it will not do. To hope that Freudian psychoanalysis will deliver us from where we are is an illusion.

As a system, it doesn't obviously work. Children educated in the light of Freudian techniques are not noticeably more imaginative or self-sacrificing or even brighter. The assump-tion that criminal behaviour is always a sickness requiring treatment leads to the excesses of *One Flew Over the Cuckoo's Nest*. More profoundly, the fundamental Freudian principle that what we are is defined by the experiences of our early childhood may make us less than human. It may make us believe that agonizing decisions of right and wrong don't really mean anything, for they are only reflections of our upbringing. We will not be delivered by psychoanalysis. No new Sigmund will get us out of the mess we're in. God had something different in mind at Bethlehem.

So perhaps Mary and Joseph might have chosen another significant name. They might have called the baby Isaac. Our best hope might be science. What the world needs is a new Isaac Newton. It could hardly be more up to date; for you will remember that Baroness Thatcher chose to put Isaac Newton on her new coat-of-arms. A strange choice, you may think, since Newton, although an admirable scientist, was a distinctly unadmirable human being. The grand passion of his life was his hostility to his rival Leibniz: to this passion he devoted remarkable talents for deviousness and vitriol; and when his rival died Newton declared that he had taken great satisfaction in 'breaking Leibniz's heart'.

No doubt Lady Thatcher knew what she was doing when she chose Newton as her standard-bearer; and he certainly was a remarkably gifted scientist. It would be reasonable to call our century the age of science. Sometimes it is biology which seems to hold out the greatest hope: from the contraceptive pill to the processing of soya beans. Sometimes it is astrophysics; or economics; or, most of all today, computers. We all live by science; and its power is everywhere to be seen. It would be no surprise if the baby to deliver us were to be called Isaac.

Yet to appeal to science to deliver us from the mess we are in is an illusion. For this century has shown that science enables us to build landmines and drug rings as much as to bring the promised land. What's more, much of the scientific enterprise works best when it reduces human beings to predictable, definable units. Which may be more ordered, but is decidedly less human; and is certainly not paradise. We will not be delivered by science. No new Isaac will get us out of the mess we're in. God had something different in mind at Bethlehem.

Really up-to-date. If Mary and Joseph had been really up-to-date the child might have been called Camelot. If the National Lottery is the symbol of our day and generation then stop the world for I want to get off. It's not individuals wasting a pound or two that worries me: I think that is silly rather than immoral. What worries me, angers me, depresses me, scandalizes me about the National Lottery is what it says about the kind of nation we are becoming. If ever there was an expression of nasty, greedy, individualistic selfishness it is that we should as a nation, organized by our government, find the biggest television audience of the year for a television programme devoted to reading out six numbers in order.

I certainly fear for charities, the arts and voluntary organizations. There is plenty of evidence to suggest that, far from benefiting from the lottery, they will be the losers. I certainly fear for the poor in our society, for there is evidence that those who have least will be encouraged to lose most in the lottery. But most of all I fear for us all, made meaner, shabbier, cheaper by this national respectability given to ordinary greed. Yet hardly anyone agrees with me and countless millions watch the rubbishy programmes and the nation is helped yet again to worship money. Mary and Joseph, however, did not call the child Camelot. God had something different in mind at Bethlehem.

'He was given the name Jesus, the name given by the angel before he was conceived.' Not more psychology, nor more science nor more money. Jesus, 'God saves'. What is needed to get us out of the mess we are in is Jesus: whose work is to overcome the darkness in which we and all the human race still walk; and bring us into God's marvellous light. What we need is love that will not let us go. God's saving love in Jesus, God's saving love at Bethlehem and Calvary: that is the gospel which we may trust whatever lies ahead.

Amen.

THE TEMPTER IS MORE CLEVER

The temptation of Jesus
LUKE 4.1–13

The tempter is more clever than you are.

Actually, the devil is not real; at least not in the sense that God is real or even that you are real. But the devil can be a useful way of speaking about the power of evil, and it is a way the Bible uses. The tempter is more clever than you are. The story of the temptation of Jesus is his best shot; nothing less would do; and the story shows the cleverness. For it's not a story about the presence of distractions, but their absence. And it's not about the absence of religion but its presence.

Which is just the opposite of what you would think, and that's why I said the tempter is more clever than you are. At his best shot it is not the presence of distractions but their absence; it is not the absence of religion but its presence. We take distractions first.

You would think that the very strongest temptations are to do with sex or drink or money and you would be wrong. The tempter knows better. When he seeks to bend or break the always human Jesus he doesn't go first to the city with all its very worldly and very obvious attractions. He does the very opposite. It is out in the wilderness, where there is no one, where there is nothing. That is where he starts to whisper.

Some of our members are just back this morning from a weekend conference. It was a great success, and there was plenty of hard work. We were thinking about 'spirituality', and at one point we were asked to write down what obstacles there were in our own lives to spiritual nourishment and growth. We didn't share answers; but I'm confident that I would not be the only one who wrote down 'not spending enough time quiet and alone'. As I thought about it afterwards I was sure it was true; but also I began to reflect that spending time quiet and alone was also sometimes an obstacle to spiritual growth. Because that is where temptation is at its strongest and best.

Why should that be? Why should the tempter wait until Jesus is all alone, with none of the seductions and attractions of Vanity Fair to ensnare him? Why might Rose Street be a less dangerous place for your immortal soul than Arthur's Seat? I think it may be that when we are all alone, when there is no one to talk to but ourselves, no one to listen to but ourselves, no one to worry about but ourselves, no one to pay attention to but ourselves – it is when we are alone that we all, all lie to ourselves and deceive ourselves and distort the truth and live in pretence and it is that, that above all which makes the tempter lick his greedy fat lips and slaver with desire. He knows he has us when we give free range to our inbuilt tendency to lie to ourselves.

We see it so clearly in everybody else. It is what is always said about alcoholics, that they have an infinite capacity for self-deception. So they do. It is what is sometimes said about prisoners, that they have an infinite capacity for self-deception. So they do. But it should also be said of generals and infants and elders of the Church of Scotland; and it should certainly be said of you. An infinite capacity to lie to yourself. One day it may be to tell yourself you are a fearful disaster whom no one could ever care for. The next day it may be to tell yourself that it doesn't matter about the hurt you caused. The next day it may be to tell yourself that you are tremendously popular. And every day it is deceit and lies and never telling yourself the truth.

So no wonder the tempter comes to Jesus when he is alone. When there is nothing around to take him out of himself. When he cannot fix his mind on a church steeple or hear a Mozart sonata or play with a child, when any of these things can bring you back to truth. There, where he is alone, he's turned in on himself, the opportunities for lies are everywhere, and the tempter lusts for conquest.

I wouldn't be surprised if the place in your home where you are most vulnerable to temptation is not the bedroom nor the dining room but the bath.

So how do you deal with it? Could you get some more religion in to your life? Spend more time in church activities. 'Fight the good fight with all your might.' 'Yield not to temptation for yielding is sin.' Surely the best weapon against temptation is religion and by definition we are most exposed and most vulnerable when there is no religion around? Does that make sense?

Then the tempter is more clever than you are!

When Jesus is surrounded by the sweet, sweet smell of temptation there is religion in the air and plenty of it. The tempter is playing his best shot and he wants it to be very religious indeed. There is scripture in the air and some of it is, as the Merchant of Venice pointed out, on the devil's lips. These temptations are all about religion. 'Make stones into bread', he wheedles, 'and then they'll believe.' 'Jump off the temple roof', he coaxes, 'and then God will show his hand.' 'Worship me', he teases, 'and you can have everything you want.' It is the titanic struggle for the future of creation and the temptations are all about religion. It is not the absence of religion but its presence which endangers most.

Not the absence of religion but its presence which the tempter seeks to gorge on. How can this be? I think it is that religion can itself be a very powerful temptation; and that it can reinforce so many other temptations. Here are three examples which might help you to see what I mean.

In the televised version of *Middlemarch* there was a cold, cruel scene where a deeply religious businessman knelt in prayer at the bedside of a desperately sick old colleague. Except that the old colleague knew the truth about the source of the banker's wealth; and the prayer on the lips of that very religious man was 'Lord, I know it cannot be your will that this poor wretch should live. May your will be done'! How corrupt religion can be!

A nine-year-old boy came to school in this city recently and came to live with friends of mine. He bullied their seven-year-old unmercifully. When they spoke to him about his cruelty he said 'God has already forgiven me. I care only about him.' How corrupt religion can be!

Robert Burns' poem *Holy Willie's Prayer* follows exactly the traditional order and pattern of public prayer. Except that at every stage Holy Willie cannot resist the temptation, the hugely powerful temptation, the corrupting temptation to manipulate religion to suit his own purposes. So where the prayer should end with thanksgiving and glory to God, instead it ends:

> But, Lord, remember me and mine
> Wi' mercies temporal and divine
> That I for grace and gear may shine,
> Excell'd by nane!
> And a' the glory shall be thine –
> Amen! Amen!

Do you see how powerful religion can be? How corrupting religion can be? The tempter is more clever than you are, because he knows that it is not the absence of religion but its presence which gives him his best chance. The most vulnerable place for you may not be a supermarket or a meeting of the National Secular Society. The most vulnerable place may be in church.

'Then Jesus was led up by the Spirit into the wilderness, to be tempted by the devil.' It is a moment trembling with destiny. Jesus is at his most stretched, exposed, isolated, defenceless. Surrounded by nothing, by nothing except religion. In this, his eternal moment, Jesus finds his strength only in God. Three times he answers: 'One does not live by bread alone, but by every word that comes from the mouth of God.' 'Do not put the Lord your God to the test.' 'Worship the Lord your God and serve only him.'

Do not seek the absence of distractions: seek the presence of God. Do not seek the presence of religion: seek the presence of God. Amen.

37

PARALYSED

MARK 2.1–12

You don't have to be in a wheelchair to be paralysed. I read a book about a man who could walk, but was paralysed. *The Remains of the Day* won the Booker Prize a year or two ago. It's a simple, touching, funny, sad book about a butler. He's a good butler, so good that he sees his whole life in terms of being a butler. That's what he's for: that's what he is. So the one real opportunity he ever has to marry, for example, he approaches by weighing up the advantages and the problems which might arrive in the pantry if the butler and the housekeeper became man and wife.

Stevens is defined by his job. The most telling incident is on the night of a grand banquet. Lord Darlington is entertaining the German Ambassador and Stevens' father is helping with the table duties. Suddenly, the housekeeper, whom he has decided not to marry as it might infringe his authority, comes rushing up to the butler with the news that his father has had a stroke in the kitchen.

'I only have a minute', says Stevens, 'The gentlemen are liable to retire to the smoking room at any moment.' He finds his father a dreadful colour, with a weak pulse, and no doctor near. 'This is most distressing', he says, 'Nevertheless, I must return upstairs.' 'I hurried upstairs', the story continues, 'and was in time to see the gentlemen proceeding into the smoking room. The footmen looked relieved to see me.'

The Remains of the Day is a funny book, but it's a sad book. Stevens approaches the end of his working life and there is nothing else. His relationship with Miss Kenton is governed by the question 'Would it be proper for Lord Darlington's butler to be married to such a person?' His last moments with his dying father are dominated by the need to be back in the smoking room to see to the needs of the gentlemen. All sorts of things in his life have been suppressed, weakened, never given the chance to grow. Can you see a sense in which I might call him a paralysed man? Everything to which he might turn is blocked by the iron bonds which have been imposed on his life by the high calling of butlery. He cannot move outside the old familiar tracks. Could we not call him emotionally paralysed, paralysed inside?

Just as there are those whose legs will not move – who have to sit and watch others roam at will – and know that these simple freedoms are not for them: so there are those who are imprisoned inside themselves – whose hearts and souls and emotions cannot soar free and unchecked – who never taste hilarity or triumph or release. And are these not also paralysed? Crippled in the spirit, with results as deadly as the results of physical paralysis?

Maybe you recognize what I'm talking about. But if this way of talking isn't anything to do with you, then think of some other examples. Think of the paralysis that is to do with fear. When the cobra rises from its coils and makes its swaying, hypnotic dance in front of its victim, what is it that makes the poor doomed frog or rat stand rooted to the spot unable to run for cover until the enemy is ready to strike? Is it a delight in the dance, or the enjoyment of the snake's brilliant conversation? Not at all! It is terror! Overpowering, insuperable fear. Does not fear produces all sorts of paralysis in humans as well as in frogs?

F. J. A. Hort was one of the two or three greatest Bible scholars in the world. His massive learning and depth of insight were legendary. The edition of the Greek New Testament which he made with his friend Westcott is still a standard work a century and a half later. Hort was minister of a tiny country congregation in Cambridgeshire: 25 people on a Sunday, half of them unable to read. His son has described how his father would sit in his study in front of a blank sheet of paper for hours and hours. Unable to put down a word because of sheer terror. Fear. Paralysing one of the greatest minds in England confronted by what would seem to an outsider a relatively simple task. A paralysed man.

Or, if we speak of fear and its paralysing effects, let me tell you of Paul Tournier. Tournier was a famous psychiatrist; and in a book called *The Strong and the Weak* he wrote: 'I often think that my vocation, both in the field of psychology and in the realm of the spirit is nothing but the banishment of fear . . . At the human level I have no answer. Fear is not amenable to the will . . . And, I must be honest, all these fears beset me as well . . . If we look them squarely in the face, if we bring them in faith to God, we can overcome them.'

No doubt there are those, though they are fewer than you think, who dismiss that kind of talk as humbug. But there are others, who know, who know all too wretchedly, what it is to be paralysed, paralysed by fear. Who know the sudden onset, the emptiness in the stomach, the pounding heart, which can be brought on by something as simple as an envelope addressed in a familiar hand, a quiet 'Can I have a word with you sometime?' Or by something inescapable, like confronting the fact that you are going to die, or that the world is at war. And they are those who know the terrible cost of such fear in paralysis, in loss of rational thought, in failure to act, in giving up.

If I'm right, and there are on every side people who are unable to do what they would want and be what they would want because they feel paralysed, imprisoned in mind or spirit, heart and soul: paralysed by fear, like Hort in his study, paralysed by routine, like Stevens the butler, paralysed by – well how many people are paralysed by the expectations that others, and particularly their parents, have had of them? (In the 'Peanuts' cartoon strip Linus remarks ruefully 'There is no heavier burden than having a great potential'!) If I'm right, and if you know, perhaps know to your cost, that I am right, then what are we to say to them?

40

Here's what I want to say. I want to say 'You're not so odd. You're not such a failure. You're not contemptible because you can't always cope. I'm the same. I know that same paralysis. I know countless people who are the same. So take my hand and let us walk together, crippled as we are, into a story.'

Jesus hears the roof open. Through the hole they lower a man who is paralysed. He lies on the ground, and you can hear the silence. Jesus calls him 'My son', and tells him his sins are forgiven. Then the anger starts. Against the background of complaint, Jesus makes a theological point about forgiveness. Then he says to the man 'Stand up, take your bed, and go home'. And he got up. 'Never before', they said, 'have we seen the like.'

Could we make that story our story? You and I who have been brave enough to admit to each other that there are times when we are prisoners ourselves, paralysed by something in our hearts and in our spirits? Could we make that story our story? I mean could we let that paralysed man be us? Have you the imagination to be there with Jesus with all your weaknesses? To come to him who wants to heal you, to set you free, to make you walk, run, soar, fly?!

Who can tell what happened that day in Capernaum? But it is a true story, true at least in this sense, that Jesus the healer still longs to make us whole, and that he still has the power to put new life into the withered limbs of our souls. Perhaps the fundamental message of the gospel is that we do not have to be as we are, and already God's work in us has begun, God's healing work to make us as he would have us be.

There's a modern hymn which begins:

We cannot measure how you heal
Or answer every sufferer's prayer
Yet we believe your grace responds
Where faith and doubt unite to care.

Let us pray: Lord Jesus bring your healing love. In silence we open ourselves to you in faith that you may set us free from the things that paralyse us . . . Give us your joy and peace within our souls. Amen.

EXPERT WITNESSES

One of the soldiers pierced his side with a spear, and at once blood and water came out.

JOHN 19.34

Call the first expert witness. You are Doctor Finlay, the world-famous authority on human physiology?

I am.

What, in your opinion, is the meaning of this verse in the story of the crucifixion of Jesus, the verse which says that a soldier thrust a lance into his side, and at once there was a flow of blood and water?

Normally dead bodies don't bleed, but it is possible for bleeding to take place very soon after death in abnormal physical circumstances.

Yes, yes, but what about the water?

There is a sac which is near the heart, called the cysterna chyli. It contains fluid like water.

So how could blood and water flow out together?

I can only speculate. I consider it not inconceivable that the heart of one subjected to enormous strain, physical and mental, might rupture and burst. Blood would then flow into the pericardium where it would mingle with that fluid. That rupture of the heart might lead to just the result described.

Could you put that technical evidence in simple language?

I suppose you could say that Jesus died of a broken heart.

Call the second expert witness. You are Professor Know-all,

43

writer of many large books on the history of the early church?

I am.

What, in your opinion, is the meaning of the verse in St John's gospel about the spear in Jesus' side?

Did you notice the very interesting verse which comes immediately after the verse you are asking me about? St John describes the water and blood flowing from the side of Jesus, and then goes on, 'This is vouched for by an eye-witness, whose evidence is to be trusted'. Now, isn't that interesting?

You've caught me there, Professor. Why should that be important?

Because it is exactly the sort of thing you would expect someone to say in a heated argument, in a very important debate. If I bring in some evidence which clearly supports my side of the argument, and if I can then show that my evidence is cast-iron solid, then I've knocked you cold, don't you see?

I'm not sure that I do. Do you mean that St John was writing this story as part of an argument? That the bit about the spear and the water and the blood was to prove his opponents wrong?

That's it exactly! You've got it! The whole of the fourth gospel was written polemically; it was written to defeat the arguments of those with whom St John disagreed; and this verse is a key part of his debate. That's why he underlines and authenticates it with the verse about the eye-witness. It was the docetists. That's what they were called. John wrote his book partly at least to prove them wrong. They held the belief that Jesus was never really human, never really suffered, never really died. Now if you believe that then, whether you realize it or not you are destroying the very centre of Christian faith. St John was not having any of it. For him Jesus was truly human, he truly suffered, he truly died. A spear in his side at the end of it; and blood and water flowing out.

44

Call the next expert witness, Rev. Andrew McLellan. You are the Rev. Andrew McLellan? And on what do you consider yourself to be an expert?

I am an expert on what happens in St Andrew's and St George's Church.

That's a fairly limited field of expertise, but what does what happens in St Andrew's and St George's Church have to do with this verse we're talking about? This verse about a soldier thrusting a lance into the side of Jesus and about blood and water flowing out at once?

The word that might help you to understand is 'symbol'. John's gospel is peppered with 'symbols'; with clues to help us tie together the life of Jesus with the life of the church and our own lives. In this verse 'water' and 'blood' are two powerful symbols. Put them side by side and what do they point to in the life of the church? What must they point to? What is so obvious about this verse that once I have said it you will never forget it? Water – what must that be? Blood – what must that be? Two symbols at the cross – the two great sacramental acts of the church. It is that blood which flows into the communion cup. It is that water which fills this font.

What this verse is doing is rooting the sacrament of baptism in the cross of Jesus Christ. The power of baptism flows from his death. Baptism brings the suffering and death of Jesus and all its benefits into the lives of those who are baptized. As the Bible itself says, 'When we were baptized into union with Christ Jesus we were baptized into his death'.

So as an expert on what happens in St Andrew's and St George's I'm here to say that, odd as it may appear, it is perfectly right and good and biblical to have the baptism of a baby on this Sunday, on this Passion Sunday when we think especially of the crucifixion of Jesus, For the crucifixion of Jesus is not just another story of tragedy and waste. It is power and life and healing: and it is all of these things for this baby here today.

Call the next expert witness. Who are you and what is your subject?

My name is X and I am an expert in nothing.

How odd! What good is that to us? We are trying to understand this verse? How can someone who is not an expert help us?

Perhaps because I could tell you my story. You will never understand God's purpose for you or God's love for the world until you realize that your story is as important as anyone's for God; that your faith is as important as anyone's for God; that you must not wait until you have listened to all the experts before you make up your mind. For you will never know what all the experts say.

Yes yes! Very fine talk. But I don't have time for that sort of stuff! What can you tell us about the text?

If you listened and I told you my story you would know that it is a story of suffering. I don't think that makes me special. Just the opposite. I think it makes me human. But it makes it easier for me to share the story of Jesus. Yes, to share the story of Jesus. I don't know how it works, but I feel, I believe, sometimes I know that the story of his pain is my story; and the story of my pain is his story.

But what does that have to do with our text?

The verse says that when Jesus was crucified blood and water flowed from his side. I think that blood and water are for me. I think they are hope out of despair, light out of darkness. I think that his death is life for me. I do not pretend to understand it at all, but I am convinced that the crucifixion of Jesus makes it all right, all right at the deepest level, all right for the universe, and all right for me. The blood and water are about cleansing, renewing; making clean, making new. That is what flows from the cross of Jesus: flows for me, and flows for the world.

What did you say your name was?

I could be anyone. I could be you. Amen.

LOCKED

Easter evening
JOHN 20.19–31

Doors locked are what you would not expect; and doors locked are what you get. Quite clearly what you get: for St John tells us not once but twice in these Easter stories that the doors in the Upper Room were locked. Which is what you would not expect.

It was the very same day, for goodness sake. Some of them had been out to the garden themselves; more dramatically, all of them by this time must have heard the story Mary had been telling. What a good story it would have made to find them sitting in the Upper Room that Easter evening with the flags out and the banquet ready and the 'welcome back from the grave' speech and the doors flung wide open! If St John had simply been a good story-teller, that would have been the story which would have proclaimed the dramatic, life-changing, revolutionary confidence of the resurrection message. But more than a story-teller, St John was writing a gospel.

The doors are locked. The bolt is pushed home, the key is turned one, two, three, four. In four ways these doors are to be seen to be locked. The doors were locked for *fear*. This is not mere apprehensiveness nor uncertainty. This is not even habitual and persistent anxiety, however destructive and paralysing that can be. This is terror. The doors are locked because their hearts are pounding and their faces are pure white. Have you ever tasted the colossal safety that closing your own front door behind you can bring? Nothing is different, the problems are as great as ever, the world won't go away, but the door is locked and stands between

47

you and whatever is out there and when you are terrified that is what matters. So it is when they are terrified that Jesus comes to them. The point John is making is clear. He emphasizes the locked doors because he emphasizes their fear. When does Jesus come? When they are afraid.

There are people here who need to hear that. It is not when they were at their best; not when they were strong; not when they were full of good humour and confidence and effectiveness. But when they could not cope; when they did not know where to turn to. It was then that Jesus Christ crucified and risen came to them and said 'Peace be with you'. 'Peace be with you.'

Doors locked for fear. And doors locked for *faithlessness*. It must be deliberate. It must be that John wants us to reflect how little they believed. There is nothing in the account of expectation, of excitement, of triumph. There is nothing to suggest that there had been only hours before the most stunning reversal of all their despair, the most startling news in all their lives, the most dramatic revelation of the faithfulness of God. God kept his promises on Easter morning, and on Easter evening it is as though they had forgotten; as though they could not believe; as though God made no difference to them. Some of them at least were believers in the morning; but by night time they were faithless together.

There is something wholly Christian about that. And something profoundly theological. It is a commonplace of Bible study that the risen Christ of the scriptures only appears to his friends. But it ought also to be a commonplace that the risen Christ appears to friends who have lost faith or who never really had faith, or to friends for whom so-called faith makes little practical difference. The locked doors are a symbol of faith forsaken. It might be that these locked doors are a sign of the gospel for you. For this is the gospel of grace. The presence of Christ does not depend on our waiting or looking or asking or believing. When there is no welcome and no expectation and no determination to be religious, Christ comes. The doors are locked because of faithlessness; and Christ comes.

The most famous religious painting in Britain is, I suppose, 'The Light of the World'. It hangs in St Paul's Cathedral and shows Christ outside a door with the words 'Behold, I stand at the door and knock'. Many a sermon has been preached on the painting of the door, which has no handle on the outside. The message is that Christ can only enter the human heart when the door is opened from the inside to let him in. Now there is a good deal of spiritual truth in that picture; but it is not the whole story. For there are times – thank God there are times – when the other symbol is the one which matters. The symbol of St John's Easter story and the locked door and through it the coming of Christ among them. Sometimes the faithfulness of God matters more than all our unfaithfulness.

Doors locked for *mystery*. At the very least we can say this is not normal. People do not walk through locked doors. When John mentions that the doors are locked, when he mentions it not once but twice, this is a sign of mystery. For the body of the risen Christ is real but not real. He walks through locked doors and yet he eats with them. They are to touch him yet they are not to touch him. He is visible and then he is no longer visible. It is extremely ambiguous. He is not as he was. Yet he is clearly not a ghost. Mystery. But mystery just where it might be expected. Is not the whole point that this presence of the one who was dead is quite unlike any other presence? It is not that he has somehow reversed death: but that he is alive for ever. He is not to die again. They have no experience to which this can be compared. We have no experience to which this can be compared. No wonder the words which are used are strange and haunting and mysterious.

This is highly theological. There is no other way for St John to make his central Easter point. For the point he wants to make is itself a paradox. The risen Christ is the one whom they knew and walked with and lived with and loved and saw crucified. There is identity from Friday to Sunday. Yet the risen Christ is not as he was. He is not to die again; he has entered into larger life. There is a new beginning between

Friday and Sunday. The thing itself is full of mystery. St John is right to surround his account with that same sense of strangeness and profundity.

Finally, doors locked for *majesty*. There is a tremendous note of authority in the Upper Room stories. What is a mere locked door to him? He comes and fills the room with his presence and his words and his new life and, yes, his majesty. His words 'Peace be with you' are not just a pious wish, nor a polite way of saying 'Hello'; they have the ring of a command. This is one who rules, and peace is his to give, and peace is his gift.

The marks of his authority are plain for all to see. His hands and his side bear all the insignia he needs. This is crucified majesty; but it is still majesty for all that. St Thomas's reaction at the second Upper Room appearance is authentic: 'My Lord and My God.' If locked doors are as nothing, might not faithlessness and fear themselves come to submit to his mystery and his majesty? If locked doors are as nothing, might not even the darkness of human hearts be lit up by his mystery and his majesty?

Long before Holman Hunt's painting was placed in St Paul's, the Dean there had a gift for poetry. John Donne knew where the most redoubtable locked door was to be found:

> Batter my heart, three person'd God; for you
> As yet but knock, breathe, shine and seek to mend;
> That I may rise and stand, o'erthrow me and bend
> Your force, to break, blow, burn and make me new,
> . . .
>
> . . .
> Take me to you, imprison me, for I
> Except you enthral me, never shall be free
> Nor ever chaste, except you ravish me.

Amen.

Part 3

Preaching about people

FROM GRUMBLING TO TUMBLING

The birth of Samson
JUDGES 13.1–5

The Bible writers were fascinated by birth stories. And many of the birth stories are strikingly similar. Two stories with a lot in common are the story of the birth of Samson and the story of the birth of John the Baptist. Two stories with a lot in common; and if your Bible has footnotes it wouldn't take you long to be led to the story of the birth of Isaac and the story of the birth of Samuel and you would soon be saying to yourself 'What is going on here?' for you would be seeing the same features cropping up over and over again. Women who longed to be mothers, heavenly messengers, the promise of a very special boy – never a girl – what is going on here?

Maybe the repeated pattern of these stories of miraculous births conceals deep truth hidden in ancient fable: deep truth which we must work to reveal.

In the story of the birth of Samson, and in these other stories which I mentioned, can you hear the *grumbling* of pain? In the four stories I have mentioned, Sarah and Hannah and Elizabeth and the nameless woman who is Samson's mother all long to have a baby and it does not happen. Last month one of our leading journalists wrote of her 'bone-crushing sadness of being childless at forty'. It is impertinent for a man and a father to say more; but the Bible does not turn its eyes away from deep human pain.

Listen to the grumbling of pain on a wider scale as well. Each story tells of a birth when things are in a mess. To Abraham and Sarah there is no sign of the promised blessing of God. In our story the Philistines have ruled the land for

52

forty years and no one in Israel does what is right in the eyes of the Lord. Read these birth stories and you hear the grumbling of pain which we heard recently when Mary Robinson, the President of Ireland, visited Somalia and then climbed on the homeward plane and wept and wept; where small nations yearn for self-determination and no one listens; where a homeless sixteen-year-old girl arriving in Edinburgh will become a prostitute in one week – guaranteed. Listen to these Bible stories, listen to the world, and hear the grumbling of pain.

Then hear the *rumbling* of hope. The repeated pattern in all of these stories is a pattern of new beginning, of new life, of hope. In every case the Bible proclaims God's determination to bring eagerness to the hopeless and healing to those in despair. The story is not about an angel; it is about God and the will of God and the hearing of the grumbling of pain and the beginning of the rumbling of hope.

But the rumbling of hope that I want you to feel in these stories is much more than the birth of a baby. It is order coming out of chaos in the beginning; it is a tiny family of wandering nomads being told they will be a great nation; it is the shaking of the walls of a temple as a crowd exults in the hundredth psalm. The rumbling of hope I want you to feel in these stories is a man's voice saying that he has come to seek and save those who were lost. It is the new creation of the world against the tyranny of death when that same man staggers out of the tomb to bright Easter light. The rumbling of hope is God himself.

Then see the *humbling*: the humbling of ordinariness in these stories. After all, what is more ordinary than the birth of a baby? Never that to parents, of course; or to obstetricians; or to theologians. And yet . . . it is not hard-hearted to say that the birth of a baby is the most ordinary thing that can happen to a person. Being born is the one thing that absolutely every one of us has done. Since I began preaching this sermon 1,500 babies have been born: what could be more ordinary than that?

In which humbling of ordinariness there is a severe

53

theological lesson. Look for God in a mighty empire and you find a bush burning in a desert to summon someone with a stammer to rescue a bunch of slaves. Look for God in a palace and the star will lead you to a stable. Look for Christ exalted in glory and if you read your Bible you'll discover that first you must read that 'he made himself nothing, assuming the form of a slave. Bearing the human likeness, sharing the human lot, he humbled himself, and was obedient, even to the point of death, death on a cross!' Look for God in the face of your neighbour and you learn that it is in the faces of the poor and hungry, the sick and those in prison, that you are to look. If a lovely church and splendid music have a danger, it is that they will distract us from seeing the ordinariness, the humbling of the ordinariness of God.

Next in these Bible stories about birth will you share the *stumbling*, the stumbling of vulnerability. It is very marked in our story about the birth of Samson, but it is there in them all. The stumbling of vulnerability. What could be more of a risk than the birth of a baby? A huge risk physically; and a huge risk emotionally, morally, psychologically. So in our story, this little boy has to be supported, protected. He is very vulnerable, and God's plans for him are very vulnerable. I am sure that is the point of the strange conditions which are imposed on Samson's mother before he is born. All these rules about alcohol and haircuts which sound to us so odd – to the Bible writers they emphasized how vulnerable, how precarious, is the birth of a baby: and in these stories that means how vulnerable, how precarious, is the work of God.

It can never be otherwise with love. Love is always vulnerable, precarious, stumbling. We could do with being a little less judgemental about royal marriages. For everyone love is always vulnerable. It is the denial of that which makes rape such a peculiarly repulsive crime. If you have ever been a teenage child trying to handle the complications of emerging from the love of the family you'll know what I mean. If you've ever tried to say prayers you will know how stumbling love is. And if you had ever been God you would know how vulnerable, how easily hurt, love is. How often in the Bible

God seems to pin his hopes on the most feeble shoulders. The stumbling of vulnerability.

Grumbling, rumbling, humbling, stumbling – and then *tumbling*. The tumbling of faith! The story of the birth of Samson goes on to a strong and encouraging scene of belief, acceptance and obedience. The woman believes the message she has been given, she accepts it for herself, and she faces up to her new obligations. She went for it. She committed herself to God and what she believed to be his will; and despite all her uncertainties and fears she went on – she tumbled in to faith.

I've quoted before from Sir Peter Parker's *Rules for Managers*. One of them is 'Do all your sums; look hard; but don't forget you still have to leap'. If you were making up rules for Christians, you might need something like that. There never comes a time when everything is clear. There never comes a time when you have the problems of suffering and world religions and what the cross means and 'can you trust the Bible?' sorted out. These are necessary questions: I am the last one to scorn a questioning approach. But there never comes a time when you have them all cracked. Either you die still looking before you leap; or you try believing; you have a shot at letting God love you. You resolve to make your life not your own but God's. You tumble in to faith and trust.

Isaac, Samson, Samuel, John the Baptist. Birth stories in the Bible. The grumbling of pain, the rumbling of hope, the humbling of ordinariness, the stumbling of vulnerability, the tumbling of faith.

Now you know what St Luke expected you to know before you read his story. His story about another birth; about an angel coming to a girl in Nazareth called Mary. Luke's story which ends with the words 'Behold, the handmaid of the Lord; be it unto me according to thy word'. Amen.

MARY

LUKE 1.26–38

My post-bag shows that this year alone I have managed to offend people by preaching about nuclear weapons, about homosexuality, and about what I mean by family values. Today's sermon is about Mary. Almost anything I say about Mary is bound to offend somebody. Roman Catholics on the one hand and radical feminists on the other may ask what right I have to say anything at all about her. Let us start with the Queen of Heaven.

Most Protestants probably find devotion to Mary the strangest part of Catholic religion. Titles like Our Lady, the Star of the Sea, the Mother of Mercy, the Queen of Heaven generally sound very odd; and it may be that the technical, theological problem is the least of it. The technical problem is about how God saves people, about how God's will is done. Protestants believe that Catholic theology tends to give Mary some special place in the salvation of the world, in the actual process of atonement. The technical reason they resist that is, at its best, not to do with hating Mary but with loving Jesus Christ. It is a determination that nothing and no one will undermine or supplant or take the place of Jesus Christ and his cross and resurrection in the purposes of God.

But does the Roman Catholic Church believe what Protestants think it believes? Deeper perhaps then the technical theological discussion is simply the strangeness, the lack of understanding, the failure to talk together. I have spent all my life at ecumenical meetings and gatherings and

56

I have never talked with Catholics about Marian theology. So everything I know about what Catholics think about Mary I have heard from Protestants or read in Protestant books. In one of the books of my old teacher of theology, John Macquarrie, however, I have read this: 'A renewed theological consideration of the issues involved will increasingly lead Protestants to abandon their negative attitudes toward Mary, and to join with their Catholic brethren in a glad Ave Maria!'

Maybe there are undiscovered treasures in Catholic attitudes to Mary that could be very good for us. But even if John Macquarrie is right and we need to do more theological work I will still be left with a different kind of problem about Mary and the way she is perceived by many of the world's Christians. The very titles tell a story: Queen of Heaven, the Mother of Mercy and so on; so does the art world. Titian's wonderful painting 'The Assumption of the Virgin' is a classic both of Renaissance painting and of Marian theology, for it shows Mary being received into heaven in triumph: leaving crowds on earth longing and bereft, passing through cheering cherubs to be received in triumph and exaltation by the Holy Trinity waiting to crown her.

It is a wonderful painting, but is it Mary? Is this Mary of Nazareth? Is this the one who is marked, distinguished, almost defined in the gospel stories by her ordinariness? There is something disturbing about the change in emphasis from being 'nobody' – as she is in the story we read from the Bible – to being the one whose glorious triumph and crowning is attended by all the exultant angels of heaven. The ordinary village girl is more authentic, she is Mary: and it is that tradition of ordinariness which is her gift to us all and which is obscured and in danger of being destroyed in the traditions of veneration which see her robed and enthroned.

Years ago in this church I heard a lecture about Christianity which was about 'the fundamental calling to be no one in particular'. That could have been a lecture about

57

Mary: it wasn't her achievements, it wasn't her goodness, it wasn't her faith, it was what God did with her, what she and God did together. Now that could really be the gospel for all of us who are called, yes, called to be no one in particular.

But now we must pause; because now the ice is becoming quite thin. A few more sentences and I will be giving a different kind of offence to a different group of people altogether. The emphasis on the ordinariness of Mary is, I believe, of enormous importance. But I am also aware that that emphasis is the hottest of hot potatoes, and could very easily become something quite wicked: indeed has in the past often become something quite wicked. I'm not talking any longer about Roman Catholic/Protestant divisions. This is something which goes even deeper; and may be more personal to us all.

Last week I bought a book by the theologian Margaret Hebblethwaite, who gave that lecture I attended here a few years ago. In this book she writes specifically about the 'ordinariness' of Mary: and this is what she says: 'The ordinariness of Mary has also been misused for more sinister purposes, to bolster up male fantasies about the ideal of the simple, uneducated, unambitious, contented woman who finds all her fulfilment in being a wife and mother.' All of a sudden the discussion about Mary has a very contemporary sound, and whatever I say is likely to fill my post-bag with more than Christmas cards.

But I must say this. If Mary has even surreptitiously or unconsciously been used by men to keep women in their place then I want nothing to do with it. I want nothing to do with it both in terms of the contemporary feminist debate; but also because of my understanding of the New Testament. In the current debate about the role of women the question is not whether it can be good and fulfilling for a woman to find her life's role as a wife and mother; very few people would dispute that. The question is whether it is only as a wife and mother that a true woman can find her life's role: and that women whose lives take other shapes are somehow lesser, or unsound, or unfortunate or disloyal or worse. That position cannot be justified and it is quite wrong for Mary to be thrust down women's throats as the supreme model in that way.

It is quite wrong because that is not what the Bible stories of Mary are about. The Bible stories about Mary are about God and God's will for her and her response to God, sure enough. But to read them as stories of a submissive woman who learns that the female principle is doing what you are told is a travesty. The breakthrough is to discover that Mary and her response are not just female models, they are models for all human behaviour. Just as I don't allow the Roman Catholic Church to own Mary, so I don't allow women to own her. She is a model for men as well as women.

The key sentence is her response to the angel Gabriel. She hears the news that she is to give birth to the Messiah. Her words are 'Behold the handmaid of the Lord: be it unto me according to thy word'. Or, 'Let your will be done in me; I will serve you in any way you want'. That is not submissive, accepting femininity. That is faith. It is commitment to the will of God. It is obedience. It is the necessary, the key, the essential human response before the power of God. That it should first be made by a woman is for women and men alike a source of wonder. But it is not an escape clause for men; nor is it a prison-house for women.

In this sermon, then, first I resist Mary the Queen of Heaven in the name of Mary the ordinary person, the one who followed 'the fundamental calling to be no one in particular'. Second, I resist Mary the model woman in the name of Mary the human being. Confronted with the invasive love of God, her wonderful courageous answer of faith belongs to us all: 'Let your will be done in me: I will serve you in whatever way you want.'

Margaret Hebblethwaite's book, *Six New Gospels*, imagines Mary as part of the early church, telling the story of Jesus, sharing her experience. It ends with Mary saying 'But though I am always busy, going where my health permits to tell my memories, and welcoming those who

come to our house to hear my story, I have the peace of mind
of knowing that my life's work is done. It was finished that
day on Calvary, when I held my dead son in my arms
and offered him to God for the salvation of the world.'
Amen.

WHAT KIND OF ROCK?

You are Peter, the Rock; and on this rock I will build
my church.
MATTHEW 16.18

Every single time the disciples are mentioned, his name comes first. When the church was struggling out of the chrysalis in the earliest days in Jerusalem after the death of Jesus, he was the undisputed leader. His importance for one section of the church ever since (and, by implication, his importance for Protestant–Catholic relationships) can hardly be overstated. Jesus calls him 'The Rock'.

The study of rocks is part of geology. Jesus did not know any geology: just as he could not speak Portuguese or ride a bicycle. But the modern science of rocks might illuminate the meaning of Jesus' nickname even if its principles cannot have been in Jesus' mind. Scientific analysis classifies rocks into three groups. They can be igneous, sedimentary or metamorphic. Which was Peter?

Igneous rocks are the result of the cooling and solidification of molten matter in the earth's interior. Deep below the surface of the earth fierce white-hot liquids seethe and bubble. Sometimes they explode out of the mouths of volcanoes with devastating results; but mostly they scald and boil in a subterranean cauldron literally as hot as hell. When some of that molten matter is separated from the burning sea for one reason or another it cools and solidifies into the hardest adamantine rock: granite is a good example of igneous rock.

Could that be Peter? A rock formed out of the seething turmoil, the white-hot explosions within. There is a painting by van Gogh, 'Starry Night', and it is a swirling, climactic production of light and power, blues and golds and circles and movement. But anyone who sees it is not surprised to learn that it was painted in a hospital for the mentally ill, for the very power of the painting so clearly is born of the inner torment, anguish and ecstasy which consumed him in the deepest places.

There are less extraordinary examples on television on Sunday nights at the moment. *Lipstick on Your Collar* is like all of Dennis Potter's writing, in that it shows us people whose outer life is humdrum, repetitive and ordinary; but whose inner life is tormented and frightening and volcanic.

Could that be Peter? Do you remember Peter near the end of the gospel story? They are in the garden of Gethsemane, and the soldiers and temple police have come for Jesus. In a flash Peter draws his sword and attacks: he injures the servant of the high priest. In the crisis, the volcano explodes. Could that even be you?

The second type of rock is sedimentary. Sedimentary rocks are formed by the gradual consolidation of particles of older rocks: chips, gravel, sand, dust coming together over long centuries to form new rock. Sandstone, coal and iron ore are examples.

Could that be Peter? A rock formed from pieces of the past? Built up bit by bit from all that has gone before? In a sense that is all of us. The new science of human genetics has clarified how each one of us has in us the genes of parents, grandparents and distant ancestors. The slightly older science of psychology has shown how the behaviour of each of us is powerfully determined by what happened to us when we are very young. Peter's past must have made him what he was.

More specifically, you can see how being Scottish, for example, might form your character, as you receive from the past a particular culture of Culloden and shipbuilding and George Street. You can see it in Christianity. We hear pretty regularly about the Disruption of 1843, that watershed moment for Scotland and Scottish Christianity which took place here in this building. To go further back, some of the congregation have been learning about Celtic spirituality. We've been examining these magnificent free-standing crosses on the Western Isles, we've been hearing the stories of Columba, and we've been discovering how the unique and attractive character of Celtic Christianity still touches the faith of us who are its heirs fifteen centuries later.

Could that be Peter? A rock formed from his past? How could it be otherwise for a Jew of all people, when from his boyhood he must have heard the stories, the stories of the deliverance from Egypt and King David and the building of the Temple? Do you remember that strange, holy moment on the Mount of Transfiguration, when the great ones of the past, Moses and Elijah, seem to talk with Jesus, and in his excitement Peter blurts out some stuff about shelters for them? So anxious to make living contact with his own past and the past of his people: to stand firm on the traditions given to him. Could that even be you?

The third type of rock is metamorphic. This kind is formed by change. Extreme pressure or extreme heat sometimes forces irreversible change in igneous or sedimentary rocks, and something new is produced. Marble and slate are examples.

Could that be Peter? A rock formed by transformation? The prestigious international prize for distinguished contribution to religion, the Templeton Prize, was awarded to Charles Colson. Charles Colson is the founder of Prison Fellowship, an evangelical organization which works to bring the healing and hope of Christ to prisoners. Twenty years ago he was for a few brief months one of the most famous men in the world, for he was President Nixon's lawyer. They used to say he was one of the toughest, most unprincipled members of Nixon's inner circle, and when Nixon fell, Colson fell too. He fell into prison: and his autobiography, *Born Again*, tells a remarkable story of a changed life as the closing of the iron doors led to the opening of doors into Christian faith.

How often have you heard someone say, in less dramatic circumstances, 'Things were never the same again' – for good or ill? Could that be Peter? In the story which is our text he faces Jesus and says 'You are the Messiah, the Son of the living God'. It is the first time in the New Testament anything quite like that is said. There is no doubt that the gospel writers meant it to be a dramatic encounter, a turning point. A moment that changed things. Could that even be you?

There is much disagreement about Jesus' response to Peter in that moment of encounter. 'You are Peter the Rock, and on this rock I will build my church.' For some it is Peter's faith which is the rock; for some it is Peter's authority. But most likely it is simply Peter himself, the first of countless believers in Christ. At this moment Jesus recognizes in Peter his first follower. One of the greatest of the early expositors of the Bible, Origen, said about our text 'Rock means every disciple of Christ'. 'Rock' might mean you.

Peter the igneous rock, boiling with inner turmoil. Peter the sedimentary rock, fulfilling his inheritance. Peter the metamorphic rock, turning around and being made new. If there is any sense in which Peter is the representative, the type, of follower of Christ; if in any one or in all of these rock forms he might be you; then you need to hear one more thing.

I said earlier that Peter's name comes first in every single list of the apostles. But there is a more precious distinction for him. The very last story in the gospels is a story about Peter, and in that story above all Peter stands for us all. The crisis is over, and in the gentle light of resurrection dawn Jesus has breakfast with his friends. Among them is the one who denied him: when it really mattered Peter turned his back. Jesus speaks to him: 'Peter, do you love me?' Peter finds his failed past given back to him forgiven and loved; and the building of the church of Jesus Christ has begun. Amen.

Part 4

Preaching about world poverty

TYCHICUS

I have sent Tychicus to you . . . that he may encourage
your hearts.
COLOSSIANS 4.8

Tychicus! He's just the boy! He's the one they need! He's a very slight figure in the Bible, but perhaps the very one we need today. On the two occasions when the Bible mentions him apart from simply recording his name, it says the same thing about him. In both the letter to the Ephesians and the letter to the Colossians the writer says to Christians who need help 'I have sent Tychicus to you . . . that he may encourage your hearts'. Isn't that nice? The one thing that is remembered about this slight figure is that he could be relied on to put fresh heart into people who needed it.

Can you picture the writer of this letter – possibly Paul, possibly not? Can you picture this writer worrying about the Christians at Colossae? For things were not easy there. They were having theological disputes, they were under pressure from outside, they were aware of the huge responsibilities that were theirs as the people of God in a pagan and needy city. So how could Paul help them? A sermon? A letter? That's not what they really need . . . I know! Tychicus! He's just the boy! He'll put fresh heart into them! So he writes 'I have sent Tychicus to you'.

Tychicus, thou should'st be living at this hour
St Andrew's and St George's hath need of thee.

If he could have been sent to St Andrew's and St George's today, what would he say to us? What would he do for us, turning now to the huge physical, emotional and spiritual effort of Christian Aid? What would he say to us, to so many

66

of whom the hill looks steeper than ever and the legs seem weaker than ever? What would he say to us, to so many of whom Christian Aid, and even Christian Aid in St Andrew's and St George's, means little or nothing? What would he do for us, this Tychicus who could be relied on to put fresh heart into those who need it? From where is encouragement to come?

Let Tychicus, let me, let the Holy Spirit of God put fresh heart into you first by emphasizing the crisis which faces us. It's Winston Churchill, offering nothing but 'blood, toil, tears and sweat'. It's Jesus, saying 'no one who puts hand to plough and then looks back is fit for the kingdom of God'. It's the hard sell, the deliberate call to struggle, 'telling it like it is'. It's the conviction that nothing is more likely to bring out the very best in a human being than the realization of impending disaster.

It is an unforgettable moment in *Les Misérables*, a moment which makes my neck tingle however often I have listened to it. The young revolutionaries have manned the barricades believing that their cause is the cause of freedom and justice, and believing that all Paris is with them. The message comes to them that they are on their own, the city is asleep, they are doomed; and immediately these young boys hurl back their defiance in glorious, magnificent heroism: *Damn their warnings, damn their lies. They shall see the people rise.*

World poverty is worse than ever. Take international debt. The Philippines owes over 34 billion dollars to the rest of the world, and just paying the interest on the debt accounts for nearly *40 per cent* of that country's annual budget. In Guatemala the fighting may have stopped, but there are still hundreds of thousands of people homeless in the hills and afraid to come out. In the Sudan it is millions. Millions facing starvation this year because of civil war and poor harvests. World poverty is worse than ever. It's hardly worth going on. It's only a drop in a bucket. They are bound upon a wheel of death – and we are impotent.

Damn their warnings, damn their lies. They shall see the people rise. Damn their warnings, damn their lies, they shall see the

67

people rise in St Andrew's and St George's in the next three weeks. In the next three weeks is there not some heroism in you? If Tychicus were here, would it not be thus he would put fresh heart into you. Courage! That is what we need. Not many of us have been called to be heroes at D-Day. Few of us have the opportunity to be heroes rescuing children from burning houses. But in the fight against world poverty, in the fight against world poverty, this is your moment!

Tychicus would also, I think, want to have a word with each of us quite personally. You can't just put heart into a whole congregation; you need to encourage each one. There is a famous story of Napoleon faced with the disaffection of his marshals: their total loss of confidence in him in the face of failure. One by one he sent for them. As each resentful, disappointed man came in to the general's presence Napoleon stood up, held out his hand, and said not a word. Every single marshal left the tent ready to die for France.

Recently I was listening to Sheila Cassidy, the doctor who made world headlines when she was tortured in a Chilean jail. She told 1,800 women about these terrible months. 'I was very scared', she said, 'and my instinct was to pray to get out; but I came to realize I was to pray to serve God there. It was as if years ago, I had signed a cheque marked "Pay God – my life"; and this was God cashing that cheque.'

Not many of us have been there; and not many of us would use such powerful language. But for all of us, each one of us, there are personal things going on. Each one of us today at our own personal stage of obedience and faith; each one of us with our own weaknesses and fears and illnesses and hurts. Each one of us with our own prayers and doubts and convictions. Each one of us different. And to each one of us, personally, Jesus says 'My grace is sufficient for you'. For you as you are. For you, the all-sufficient grace of Jesus Christ. I don't know what gifts of oratory or personality Tychicus had. But I do know that he could have no message more encouraging, no message better for putting fresh heart into people, than that saying of Jesus, 'My grace is sufficient for you'.

Perhaps Tychicus spoke of the coming crisis to put fresh heart in them. Perhaps Tychicus spoke of Christ's personal relationship with each of them to put fresh heart into them. And perhaps – no, certainly – he spoke to them of the presence of God. It is that, that above all, that I want to speak of as we move in to these final, frantic and fearful days of preparation for Christian Aid. In the other New Testament letter which mentions Tychicus as an encouraging person, Ephesians, there is a well-known passage about the armour of God. Maybe it was that very picture that Tychicus took to Ephesus to put fresh heart into them. We are to put on the presence of God like a suit of clothes. Like a suit of armour to fight in the struggle against evil and disease and poverty.

> Stand therefore, and fasten the belt of truth around your waist, and put on the breastplate of righteousness. As shoes for your feet put on whatever will make you ready to proclaim the gospel of peace. With all of these, take the shield of faith . . . Take the helmet of salvation, and the sword of the Spirit.

Most likely Tychicus would speak to them of the presence of God by telling stories of Jesus. It was much harder for him, of course. He had no New Testament! How could he have? Since he was taking part in it! We cannot tell if he knew the story of Jesus calming the storm. We cannot tell if he knew of Jesus healing the paralysed man. We cannot tell if he knew of the saying of Jesus with which St Matthew's gospel ends: 'Be absolutely certain, I am always with you.' We cannot tell whether he knew these things. But we do. They are ours to lean on and draw strength from. They are ours to put fresh heart into us.

What Tychicus would definitely use when speaking to the Colossians of the presence of God would be his Bible, their Bible, the Old Testament, the only Bible they had. I wouldn't be surprised if he read to them the Old Testament passage in Joshua chapter 1. After all, the Bible does call him a minister; and minister after minister since, including this one, has trusted in that Old Testament text to encourage those who are fearful. It is the word of God to Joshua as he faces the biggest task of his life, and I would want it to be the word of God to us all as we face the next three weeks:

> I hereby command you: Be strong and courageous; do not be frightened or dismayed, for the Lord your God is with you wherever you go.

Amen.

GARDEN THEOLOGY

The Lord God planted a garden . . . and in it he put the man
he had formed.
GENESIS 2.8

G. K. Chesterton suggested that the most important question you could ask a seaside landlady when prospecting for holiday accommodation was 'What is your view of the universe?' Not 'How often do you change the sheets?' nor 'Do you turn eggs when frying them?' but 'What is your view of the universe?' The idea was that if she got her theology right she would be likely to get the clean sheets and the bacon and egg right. I want to suggest that we make a mess of the planet earth because we get our theology wrong and to suggest that the single most useful thing we could do in the face of the environmental disaster, the disaster of world poverty, the threats to world peace which roar their hot and smelly breath into our faces until we will soon be able to ignore them no longer – the most useful thing we could do would be to learn a little theology.

I say that particularly on this day when we dedicate our Christian Aid help forms and begin the last big push up to the exhausting moments before Christian Aid Week. And I say it particularly in a week when the Prince of Wales has been drawing attention to the world summit conference on the care of the planet which will be attended by the Prime Minister in Rio de Janeiro in June. One of our members spoke movingly a few weeks ago here about the importance of that conference and our support of it: in a week or two I will offer you an opportunity to pledge yourself to the care of the earth.

But I say that the most useful thing you could do about the care of the planet and all its people would be to become a better theologian; and I say it deliberately in response to the conviction of Jonathon Porritt, the most articulate voice of green concern in Britain, that Christianity is the arch-enemy of the new green enlightenment. Porritt's hostility to Christianity is a theological one: he believes it to be the enemy of proper environmental concern because of the 'central Christian axiom that nature has no reason but to serve man'.

His argument against Christianity is a theological one. If you believe that the Bible teaches that God has given us the world to do what we like with: if you believe that the world is simply there for our benefit, then you can plunder and rape it without any thought – without any thought beyond the self-interest of protecting its resources so that there will still be plenty of opportunity for plunder and rape in the years to come. If God has no dream for the planet beyond its usefulness to us then let's get stuck in to the rainforests and blow up a few oil-wells and build lots more nuclear warheads and keep the city lights burning all night. If the planet is there for us then it is our duty, our Christian duty, to get the most we can out of it.

And the theology behind it – here we come to the heart of the matter – is in the Book of Genesis: 'God said let us make human beings to have dominion over every living thing that moves on the earth.' Perhaps that verse has encouraged us to think that it is Christian to exploit the things of the earth.

One illustration of what I mean among hundreds is the fate of the American bison. For centuries they roamed in vast herds on the North American plains providing food and clothing for native Americans. The arrival of Christian-influenced white people in the West who killed them for the delicacy of their tongues and shot them for sport from trains was cataclysmic. In 1800 there were 60 million bison in America; by 1860 the creature was all but extinct.

Jonathon Porritt argues that the theology led to the exploitation; and the more sensitive among you might feel that the most appropriate response is not a few clever debating points, but horror, shame and repentance.

Do you see how vital it is to get your theology right? And how the single most useful thing you could do for the planet would be to be a better theologian? It is of supreme importance for Christians to find a theology of the earth which will allow us all to live.

For that theology you still start in the Book of Genesis. Genesis contains two creation stories. One is the seven-day account of Genesis chapter 1. This is the account, with its apparent Big Bang theory, which has been receiving some rather misguided support as a result of discoveries by American astronomers at present. And it is from this account that the words about human dominion over the earth come: the words which have provided some kind of justification for greed and exploitation. But Genesis chapter 2 contains a different story of beginnings: equally biblical, equally important for theology, but different. This is the story of Adam and Eve. This story offers us another way in to doing theology of nature; and if we could get this theology right – well, that might be about the most useful thing we could do.

At the beginning of the story in Genesis chapter 2 we read: 'The Lord planted a garden . . . and in it he put the man whom he had formed.' A garden. A garden. Think about that as an image of the earth, of the planet, of nature. In the garden he put the man. Think about that as a relationship between the human race and the earth, as a theology of nature. Then read on in Genesis: 'The Lord God took the man and put him in the garden of Eden to till it and look after it.' 'To till it and look after it'! How different that sounds from Genesis chapter 1, 'to have dominion over it'. How fateful for Christianity, for the West, for us all, for the earth, that 'dominion' theology has called the tune, and 'garden' theology has been suppressed.

But Genesis 2 is just as much Bible as Genesis 1. 'Garden' theology is every bit as biblical as 'dominion' theology. You would be thoroughly Christian if you trained yourself to think of the world as God's garden and our role in it as to cherish, to care for, to cultivate, to love. Does that remind you of a saying of Jesus: 'I am the true vine, and my father is the gardener'? If Jesus can speak of God as a gardener, would it not be a very high and splendid theology to think of the human race itself as placed in his garden to do his work with him? Fellow-workers with God! Gardeners all!

On the first Easter Day Mary turns disappointed from the empty tomb. She meets a strange figure, and she supposes him to be the gardener. I used to think that the most absurd mistake; but I now think it rich and full of meaning. For she is right. He is the gardener. He is the second Adam come to restore Eden. And, one of us as he is, what is he to do but to cherish and love and cultivate and heal the garden which is God's gift to the human race?

Get the theology right and you could not stay out of Christian Aid. For this is 'garden theology' put to work. Here literally by your work 'the desert will rejoice and blossom like the rose'. Here much will go wrong, and much effort will be wasted, and much that we meant to do we will not do, but some seed will fall on good soil, and will grow, and will produce a crop, and the yield will be thirty-fold, sixty-fold, even a hundred-fold. Amen.

JANE CROSS

A new command I give you: Love one another. As I have loved
you, so you must love one another.
JOHN 13.34

Her minister went to see Jane Cross on her hundredth
birthday. She had been a missionary in Africa for most of
her life; and that Christian life was drawing to a close in a
Church of Scotland Eventide Home. They had fun and
cake and prayers together; and just as the minister rose to
leave she told him she had a problem. 'You see all these
cards?' – Her hand pointed all round the room – 'well, you
can't guess how many of these cards contained more than
good wishes. Over and over again when I opened them I
found a five-pound note, or a ten-pound note. When you're
a hundred, you haven't much need for money! What could
I do with it? I would love it if somehow this money could do
some good. If it could do some good for the church I've
loved, and for the Africa I've loved.'

So her minister gave her a kiss and went away and
thought. When she added it all up it was nearly £200 she
had received in cash for her birthday. He decided to write to
the church in Africa she had been part of and to ask them
what they would like him to do with the money. He got a
surprising answer back. 'We would like you to make the
money grow! Make the money grow and send it to us and
when there is enough, here is what we will do. We will build
a tiny house: and we will rent the house and use the rent to
send three or perhaps four children to school: children who
otherwise would have no education.'

It made sense. So the minister said to himself 'How do we
make this money grow?' All he did was tell the story one

Sunday morning. After the benediction a little group waited behind and said 'Look, we know the old lady. We'd like to do something to help.' The next thing it was the Cubs, who held a sponsored eat-in. Before they stopped to think, the whole congregation, the whole town, seemed to be helping the money to grow; and it wasn't long before they sent the old lady's hundredth birthday money, all £8,000 of it, off to Africa.

Where it was a fortune. On the strength of that capital, the church borrowed more money and built a really big house; and from it there was a lot of rent. From the rent they did more building. And now Jane Cross House, in Malawi, is big enough to be a school in its own right, and in it 200 children receive education.

That happy story is rich in Christianity. You could see how it might begin a sermon on the story of the widow's mite. For without the initial generosity of the old woman nothing at all would have happened. Or the parable of the mustard seed. The modest beginning – a few £10 notes: and from it today a school for 200 children. There could be a very powerful Christian word from that story for people who are very old: who find that with the failing of their physical and mental powers there is often a sense of uselessness, which can bring with it a failure of spiritual powers as well. Is not that story of Jane Cross on her hundredth birthday a remarkable encouragement to those who say to themselves or to others 'What can I do? At my age, what can I do that will make any difference?'

Go a little deeper into the story and you find the parable of the talents. That parable is primarily an attack on religious people who like to keep the good news of God to themselves; but I think it is quite legitimate to think of it in connection with our story. That bold request from the church in Africa, 'We want you to make the money grow', at the very least reminds us of the contrast in Jesus' story between those who did absolutely nothing with what they were given, and those who put it to work. I would not want to turn that parable into an endorsement of continuous economic growth, for the

76

parable is simply not about that; but I do think the parable and the story both address to us the question 'How can I do most good with what I have?'

Or Christian Aid. Is not that the perfect story for Christian Aid? As today we give thanks to God for what God has done through us here yesterday for the world's poor; and as we remind ourselves that even the huge sum raised is microscopic in the scale of world poverty; and as we ask ourselves where we can go from here; so the story of Jane Cross is ideal for us. For that story reminds us firstly how much more good modest sums of money can do in Third World economies than they can here. The thought that a school for 200 people could grow out of an original investment of £8,000 here is ridiculous; but £8,000 can buy more in other places. The money raised here yesterday can make, will make, will make next month a real and substantial difference. Secondly, the story reminds us of the basic Christian Aid principle, that money is always spent in consultation with partners. With partner churches, with partner aid organizations on the ground. So money is spent wisely and usefully and in line with the genuine requests of the people and of the churches. Third, the story of Jane Cross sets us free from being prisoners of huge amounts. I would not want St Andrew's and St George's ever to feel that the only thing worth doing for Christian Aid is £54,000. I can envisage circumstances in which £200, or £8,000, might be every bit as precious to God as these enormous sums. God blesses a cheerful giver, the Bible says. I think it is not too much of a distortion of the text to suggest that God blesses a cheerful Christian Aid worker, whatever the total. Of course we rejoice and are humble at what happens here, but we are not to feel this scale of contribution as a burden. The burden is borne by the starving: the privilege is to be allowed to help at all.

But above all the Christianity that is in the story of Jane Cross is the Christianity of our text today. Jesus said 'A new command I give you: Love one another. As I have loved you, so you must love one another.' There is often a structural side to that text. Christian Aid is the structural side to loving one another: so is the National Health Service, so is our Sunday offering. Ways in which we are able to bring healing and hope to our fellow human beings even if we never know their names. But there is also a personal side: an engagement of the heart and mind and will. That old woman full of years and faith, with a heart just full of love for a land and for people to whom she gave all her best years. 'Love one another. As I have loved you, so you must love one another.'

Of all the sayings of Jesus, none is more daunting. Peter is to love Judas as Jesus loved them both. Make it more pointed still: Peter is to love Andrew his brother as Jesus loved them both. Thank goodness that's all in the olden days. Except it's not. I am to love each of you as Jesus loved you. Each of you is to love me as Jesus loves me. You are to love people whose politics you hate, whose values you despise, whose personalities you can't stand; you are to love people who ignore you and put you down and are cruel to you; you are to love them as Jesus loved you.

It would be laughable, if it had not been Jesus who said it. For whatever else Jesus of Nazareth was, he was one who knew the human heart. He understood what we are, and what we are not. And he said it. Knowing Peter and Andrew and Judas clearly and unromantically, he said it. Knowing you and me clearly and unromantically and accurately, he said it. 'Love one another. As I have loved you, so you must love one another.' I promise you, he would not have said it if he did not think you were up to it.

Amen.

Part 5
Preaching about the arts

OSCAR WILDE

I do not understand my own actions. For I do not do what
I want, but I do the very thing I hate . . . For I do not do the
good I want, but the evil I do not want is what I do.
ROMANS 7.19

Between 1895 and 1900 in the United States alone, 900
sermons were preached against Oscar Wilde. On holiday I
read the story of his life; and in the midst of the Edinburgh
Festival I propose to redress the balance by one!

In the midst of the festival indeed. In St Andrew's and St
George's it is Festival Time Rules O.K. These three weeks
are now a huge operation for us. 12,000 of our leaflets
distributed; a student employed full time to work with all the
volunteers; the Undercroft running all day; an enormously
successful first week culminating in closed doors and house
full notices for our church choir's splendid concert yesterday.
In the midst of St Andrew's and St George's at Festival Time
it is healthy for us to spend a little time with Oscar Wilde.

For he was much more than a clever playwright and coiner
of quotable witticisms. First and foremost he was a thinker
about art: about painting and music and poetry. He asked
'What is it all for?' 'What difference does it make?' 'Is it
supposed to make you better?' His own view was that art
contained life's secret and life's future; and he drifted away
from the Christian church because he felt that it trivialized
these great questions; because he felt that a theatre playing
King Lear was more likely to be struggling with the deepest
mysteries of life than a church going through the routines of
morning prayer. A century on I fear the challenge remains
unanswered. Despite valiant efforts by many congregations,
not least this one, to support artistic events, we are still very
timid about facing the deepest questions which Beethoven

and Ibsen put to us; and the world of the arts and the world of the Edinburgh Festival is often left to find the spirit of God as best it can.

In my holiday reading, however, I found Wilde's long shadow hovering over much more than the Edinburgh Festival. There is a poignant story near the end of Wilde's life. It's a story told by Dame Nellie Melba, the opera singer, who, with Wilde, was the toast of London society. She was in Paris late one evening when a tall lurching figure in a shabby raincoat sidled up to her and said 'Dame Nellie Melba: I am Oscar Wilde, and I am going to do a terrible thing. I am going to ask you for money.' His decline was total: and you can't read the story without anguish and anger. Two things in particular destroyed him: and both of them challenge us today.

It's well known that he was homosexual. I don't find easy some of the issues around homosexuality. There are biblical texts which don't go away; and there are questions about marriage which I find very difficult. But there are some issues about which I am absolutely clear. I am absolutely clear that the disgusting cruelty, bullying, innuendo, fear, suspicion and intolerance which form the inescapable background to the lives of many sensitive teenagers and lovable adults is a disgrace: and that any decent person ought to be ashamed of the damage done by smutty jokes and destructive gossip. I am absolutely clear that the church of Jesus Christ exists for no other purpose than to serve his loving healing accepting way – the way which 'religious' people have hated since they first heard the stories of the gospel – and that prejudice and rejection have no place among us. I am absolutely clear that stereotypes of homosexuals as promiscuous pederasts do not bear examination. Oscar Wilde was destroyed by public pathological hatred of homosexuality. Are we any better?

Maybe it's unfair to say that. For he was also destroyed by the conditions of Britain's prisons. He was sentenced to two years' hard labour, and the accounts are terrible. The sanitary arrangements, the lack of health care, the gratuitous ill-treatment, the brutal punishments for tiny misdemeanours, the meaningless and painful hard labour itself, the absence of any books, and the crass idiocy of the prison chaplains make horrifying reading. Christian Britain's system of humiliating and destroying its prisoners was totally successful with Oscar Wilde: remember that when you remember the good old days.

Of course, it's quite different now. Certainly hard labour has disappeared, but how confident are you that our prison conditions reflect the values you would want to see? Isn't the sad truth that most of us don't care what happens behind closed doors, that very, very few of us take the trouble to find out, and that only the exceptional ones among us ever try to do anything to help? This despite the clear word of Jesus that visiting those in prison is on the same level as feeding the hungry? I was chaplain in Scotland's most comfortable prison: and I used to get very angry when ignorant people would tell me that the wretched lives of these pathetic girls were just like a holiday camp. But no sane person could ever suggest that about Scotland's male prisons. Those who believe that the proper use of prisons is to make people the sort of people who will not return have sometime to stand up to those in whom the desire to punish is very strong. Would you not say that the way it treats its prisoners is a key test of a civilized society?

The Edinburgh Festival and Britain today kept interfering with my holiday book. But neither of them as much as St Paul and the seventh chapter of Romans. Wilde would know better than I the proper technical meaning of the word 'tragic': but his story is to the plain reader a classic tragedy. It begins with glittering success: a double First at Oxford, early literary triumphs, the friendship of the great and good, and an unparalleled gift for talking. And it ends in grief, disaster and loneliness. If you didn't know St Paul very well you might think the lesson is obvious: 'The wages of sin is death'; 'One reaps what one sows'.

But the real lesson of the Bible is more profound: and much nearer to each of us. For when I said that Wilde's story was a classic tragedy, what I meant was this. Over and over again, he finds himself confronted with choices: one of these choices leads to happiness and freedom, the other leads to darkness and chains. And over and over again he makes the wrong choice. Doom approaches, and still there is honourable escape. But to the very end he is driven, compelled, fated, to make the choices that must destroy him. It is almost that he is a victim of things inside himself that he cannot control, which drive him away from the good and force him to choose what is bound to be bad.

So this morning we read St Paul: 'I do not understand my own actions. For I do not do what I want, but I do the very thing I hate . . . For I do not do the good I want, but the evil I do not want is what I do.' It's as if there never was a straight choice between doing good and doing evil: that always and everywhere there is an in-built bias in all of us – in all of us, not just Oscar Wilde, not just St Paul – in all of us an in-built bias towards choosing what is wrong and dark and silly and fatal.

Is this not what psychologists are talking about when they talk of the self-destructive instinct? In dark and mysterious ways each of us intent on causing harm to our very own selves? Is this not what Oscar Wilde wrote about in his last work, the unforgettable *Ballad of Reading Gaol*?

Yet each man kills the thing he loves
By each let this be heard
Some do it with a bitter look
Some with a flattering word
The coward does it with a kiss
The brave man with a sword.

'Each man kills the thing he loves . . . The coward does it with a kiss.'

'While he was still speaking suddenly a crowd came, and the one called Judas, one of the twelve, was leading them. He approached Jesus to kiss him.' 'And they led him away . . . and when they came to the place that is called The Skull, they crucified him.'

Nowhere is Wilde's poetry 'Each man kills the thing he

loves' more painfully true than in the crucifixion of Jesus. Nowhere is St Paul's psychology 'the evil I do not want to do – this I keep on doing' more profoundly true than in the crucifixion of Jesus. But what if in that same crucifixion of Jesus the darkness which holds each of us as it held Oscar Wilde comes to the light? The pain which holds each of us comes to healing? And the doors of the prison in which all of us are held are forced apart? Amen.

WHO OWNS ART?

All round Edinburgh for the next three weeks you will hear just the music with which this service began, for Dvořák's New World Symphony is everywhere.

Who owns that? Dvořák is the star composer of this year's Edinburgh Festival and this morning's question at the very beginning of this great celebration of the arts is 'Who owns Dvořák's music?' Or Schubert's? Who owns J. S. Bach?

Who owns *Othello*? or *Tam o' Shanter*? Who owns the thrill and excitement and beauty and faith which we will share next Saturday when our church choir perform the sacred music of Henry Purcell?

That may be enough examples to persuade you that the question is a wrong question. What would be called in logic a confusion of categories. For it's a plain and obvious and essential point that no one owns art. Ownership isn't an appropriate way of speaking about art.

There was a terrific row recently about whether public money should be spent – millions of it – on Canova's statue 'The Three Graces': a statue on display three hundred yards from this building. A serious ownership story.

Or unless you were in St Petersburg last month, as Irene and I were. The chief among the many glories of that wonderful city is the Hermitage museum. One day only allows the most cursory inspection; but we were thrilled and overwhelmed. The breathtakingly memorable experience in the Hermitage this year is called 'Hidden Treasures'.

It is a huge gallery, and it is filled with paintings that no one knew existed. In Nazi Germany numbers of precious paintings had been plundered from Jewish families. The Red Army carried these off to Russia where they were stored in boxes in the basement of the Hermitage and forgotten. Completely forgotten. Until they were discovered last year and put on exhibition a few months ago. The effect is heart-stopping. Seventy-two masterpieces: Renoir, Cezanne, Monet, Picasso: each entrancing, wonderful and strangely familiar: and each being seen for the first time for fifty years.

When the exhibition opened, the Museum invited the surviving descendants of the families who owned them to come. They were understandably few in number; but they came and apparently were pleased to come. Now of course the Museum faces a very painful question. In this case the question 'Who owns art?' is frighteningly real. To whom do these priceless gems belong? That raises deep issues of history and politics and ethics. For some people it can be very painful to ask 'Who owns art?'

Whenever the question about the ownership of art does make sense it seems to throw up controversies. And that might just confirm the hint with which we began, that there is something deeply inappropriate, unhelpful, almost wrong, about applying the concept of ownership to art. And if you feel that at the beginning of the Festival, then you might be on to something important about what it means to be human; and you might be on to something central about God.

What it means to be human is to belong together. For all the political controversies over the last fifteen years about the concept of 'society' nowhere more than in the word of art can we see ourselves as belonging together. It is what *Othello* and Dvořák and 'The Three Graces' touch in all of us, bringing us together, awakening our sense of sharing together in the human race, forming the audience, the listener, the reader into a community – even if the reader or the listener is physically alone – it is that sense of including each of us in some deep shared human experience which is one of the irreplaceable gifts of art. And it is that deep common sharing which cannot be owned, cannot be copyrighted, cannot be bought and sold. Our awakening to the silliness of the question 'Who owns art?' might just help us to see how silly, how crass, how anti-human is the spirit of so much of our age: the spirit of acquisitiveness and materialism and measuring by price and having to own things. That spirit divides us off from each other, divides us into those who own and those who don't. The spirit of art, on the other hand, roams, blows, plays around us all the time: embracing, uniting, making us one. You can't own that sort of thing. Might as well talk about owning the wind.

Which is exactly what Jesus did talk about. In our gospel reading Jesus confronts Nicodemus. You can't put God where you want him. You can't own God. For the Spirit of God is like the wind. You feel and see the wind at work, but you never, never trap it, or seal it up or possess it. You can't own the wind. That's how to think of God, and the spirit of God, says Jesus. Exactly as we've been thinking of the spirit of art. Free, untameable, roaming, and never to be possessed. The Edinburgh Festival has suddenly brought us very close to one of the Bible's key convictions and we are about to solve one of the Bible's key problems.

From today you will understand what may always have puzzled you about the Bible. For we are on the brink now of understanding why the Bible rages, screams, fulminates against what it regards as just about the worst thing people can do. Have you never thought it odd that so much of the Bible, from the Ten Commandments to St Paul's climactic Letter to the Romans, spends so much energy condemning idolatry? After all, not many of us are tempted to carve little statues of God and worship them; and sometimes we feel a little superior to primitive peoples who went in for that sort of thing.

Don't you believe it! Get out of your head the thought that you are at all superior in any religious sense to the people of the Bible, who, for the most part, would leave all of us standing in terms of theological sophistication and spiritual sensitivity. Get it into your head that the Bible's fear of idolatry might be something to do with you, and that you might just grasp what is going on. The sin is not in the little doll. The sin is in the desire, the attempt, the determination to own God. The determination to own God: that is what the Bible hates. And to that temptation religious people today are as vulnerable as ever they were in the book of Exodus. When you hear in the Bible about idolatry, it is the desire to possess God, to have God at our disposal, to keep God in our pocket, which is the enemy condemned.

Trying to own God is certainly a confusion of categories; like trying to own art. But it is much worse. Trying to own God is what the Bible means by idolatry. It is idolatry when a church presumes to have God where it wants him, so that God's protection and guidance will stay with the church however perverse and disobedient that church is. That is not the God of the Bible: that is an idol and must be destroyed. It is idolatry when a nation presumes to have God on its side ready to defend it in all circumstances and crush its enemies. That is not the God of the Bible: that is an idol and must be destroyed. It is idolatry when pious people open the drawer marked 'God' morning and evening and say their prayers and spend the rest of the day doing exactly as their pleasure leads them and still expect God to be there for them in the drawer when they want him. That is not the God of the Bible, that is an idol and must be destroyed. What if the chief purpose of your God was to ease your conscience and let you off and tell you that 'it doesn't matter'? That is not the God of the Bible but an idol.

That idol, these idols are nothing. They cannot save. They cannot heal. They have no power to forgive. They cannot give eternal life. An idol cannot love. For God's sake, for your own sake, for the sake of church and nation, these tame, domestic, pet gods, these idols, must be destroyed. For they stand between us and the God who will not be possessed, or tied down or put into anyone's pocket. The God who judges and delivers us. The God who roams and moves and leaps

88

and thrusts like the wind. The God whose breath we might feel in the spirit of this Edinburgh Festival. The God who cannot be owned.

Amen.

THE STORY

The story of The Garden of Eden.
GENESIS 3.1–7

The story of The Last Supper.
1 CORINTHIANS 11.23–26

The story of The Rich Fool.
LUKE 12.16–20

In a radio interview with the Director of The Edinburgh International Festival, Brian McMaster, it was interesting, though not surprising, to hear him say 'opera is the most profound form of art': the sort of thing which you will hear endlessly argued in this city over the next three weeks; and how could you prove him right or wrong? Which is just what makes the arguing fun!

I want to put in a word for the story as an art form. I don't propose to set up Chekhov to compete with Verdi, nor Flannery O'Connor to have it out with James MacMillan; but I do want to put in a word for the story. On holiday I picked up a copy of *The Oxford Book of Short Stories*; and that set me thinking. When I came back I saw the sermon my colleague preached here last Sunday and I found that he began the sermon with a very good story; and then the first thing that someone said to me about last Sunday was to tell me the story from the sermon. Whether it is a more profound art form than opera no one can answer; but there is something universal and important about stories.

In the most precious account the Bible can make of the wonderful but spoiled relationship between God and God's children, a relationship of love and rejection, of freedom and judgement, of giving and refusing to receive, of patience and despair and pain and hope, it doesn't write a philosophical essay, it doesn't even write a poem, it tells a story. The story of the man and the woman in the garden has certainly confused millions; but it has also touched millions more, not just in their heads, not just in their hearts, but in their souls. Read the story again, and see if you do not find yourself weeping when it becomes clear to you that you are that woman, you are that man, that the whole human race of which your mother and your enemy and the Serbs and the Bosnian Muslims are a part is that man and that woman and the same story is still going on; there was never yet a more human, a more fearful, a more awesome story. Pure art.

With that kind of precedent and authority, I am encouraged to do what I nearly always try on this particular Sunday. It causes deep sighs among the discriminating, but I know that there are one or two who appreciate a couple of holiday stories. Among the varieties of Scottish rain encountered this summer by the McLellans was Iona rain. It was the day before my wife's birthday; I had no present; and I was beginning to panic. Many of you will know the shop at the Abbey and will agree that it was easy to find an attractive card. I chose that, but I could not see the right gift. Increasing agitation, consultation with the shopkeeper, whispered advice from friendly passers-by; but eventually I was so confused that I walked out of the shop. In bed that night I realized that I had left the shop clutching the birthday card, unpaid for. So I wished my wife 'Happy Birthday' with stolen property!

Then came the judgement! And when it came it was a truly biblical judgement. For on the birthday morning when I emerged onto the island street I found lying in front of me – a pound coin! So much for the stuff I tell my children – 'crime doesn't pay' – 'your sins will always find you out'. I steal a birthday card – and I am rewarded with a pound. What kind of world do we live in?

What makes that a kind of biblical judgement is just that question. What kind of world do we live in? The Bible writers are not blind to the facts. Very often wrong is rewarded and very often right does not flourish. They put the question 'Wherefore does the way of the wicked prosper?' or 'Why do bad people do so well?'

Grown-up religion does not pretend that life is fair and that everything turns out all right. It isn't and it doesn't. Real religion shouts at God and weeps and complains about the way evil goes unpunished. But somehow it insists on keeping hold of a conviction that God, for all the ups and downs of the world, is on the side of right and truth and justice; and that he is against wickedness and evil and wrong. More than that, in spite of all the success that evil seems to carry with it, somehow in the end God's will will be done and every hurt be healed. But also a biblical judgement in this: when the prodigal returned, having stolen birthday cards and worse in a far country, his father ran to meet him, kissed him, and spread a feast before him.

The writer of Genesis telling a story. My colleague here telling a story. I'm beginning to feel I'm in good company when I remember what St Paul did to teach the Christians at Corinth a lesson. Things were in a mess at Corinth with worship. Particularly with their communion services. Paul could have given them a lecture; he could have given them a row; he could have given them some tip-top theology. But what did he do? You're absolutely right!

'For I received from the Lord what I also handed on to you', he writes – it's the passage we read this morning – 'the story which I told you' 'that the Lord Jesus on the night when he was betrayed took a loaf of bread, and when he had given thanks, he broke it' . . . and so on. If you want to understand the Lord's Supper, if you want to do it right, if you want to offer to God this most precious gift, if you want to receive in it God's grace in all its fullness, then listen to the story again! The story becomes the thing itself.

Christians of all people will be the last to disparage story-telling. Christians of all people, for they know the stories of Jesus. A famous scholar said 'a parable is art'. But what he said in full was 'a parable is art harnessed for service and conflict'. The stories of Jesus are told for the express purpose of changing those who hear them. The Good Samaritan, the Prodigal Son – told for the express purpose of changing those who hear them. That brief story we read this morning, the irony of the rich man building barns to house his wealth, and never having the opportunity to enjoy it, that story is not a clever reflection on the transitoriness of life or the wickedness of greed. Rather it is a story to open people's eyes, to make it clear that the moments for decision do not last for ever, to press upon us the urgency of sorting out our lives now.

Which brings me to my second holiday story. When I was playing golf at Grantown-on-Spey I discovered this tale about the town's most famous golfer, Bobby Cruickshank. Cruickshank had tied with the legendary Bobby Jones at the end of the United States Open Championship and the two of them had to play a deciding round. Halfway through the Grantown man needed to sink a tremendously difficult putt. When he saw his ball trickle into the hole he hurled his putter exultantly into the air with a great shout of 'Thank God!' Unfortunately, he was so thrilled with the putt that he forgot – and next moment his putter landed 'thump!' on the top of his head! Poor Bobby Cruickshank was so stunned and confused by the blow that he lost hole after hole thereafter, Bobby Jones went on to take the title, and Cruickshank missed his moment – forever.

Sometimes tomorrow never comes: for golfers, for rich fools, or for those who would serve God. Stories can be very special. But in the end, what does it matter whether people say that opera or dance or story or ceramics is the greatest art? I'll tell you what does matter, what indeed I believe to be the most important thing there is. I believe that the most serious, true, and liberating answer to any of the basic questions of life is . . . to tell a story. It is a story which begins 'There were shepherds abiding in the fields, keeping watch over their flocks . . . '; which goes on 'He said, "Father, forgive them, for they do not know what they are doing"'; and ends with a doubter feeling the wounds on a man's body and whispering 'My Lord and my God'.

Except that that story doesn't end there; and cannot end until you and I and all the world are part of it. Amen.

TO BE A CRITIC

That your love may overflow more and more with knowledge and
full insight, to help you determine what is best.
PHILIPPIANS 1.9, 10

To determine what is best. When you learn that there will have
been 11,000 performances in the Festival and Fringe it is
quite important to learn to discern what is best. Learning
how to judge, forming critical assessments. It is notoriously
difficult. How do you pick a good play from the rubbish? What
marks classic ragtime? Is Allan Ramsay a great painter?

Notoriously difficult questions. I would not like to be a
critic, in spite of all the delightful free evenings they spend
at the Usher Hall. For every piece they write prompts the
question 'What do they know about it anyway?' Who is an
expert when it comes to discerning what is best? Did you
notice the death last week of John Cage? He was a leading
American composer of minimalist music. His best-known
work is called 'Four minutes and thirty-three seconds' and
consists of a pianist's sitting immobile on a piano stool with
the piano closed for precisely that length of time. So difficult
is the business of critical judgement that few dare stick their
necks out even on such an extreme example.

How to discern what is best? These words about the
critical process come from the Bible; and in the middle of
the Festival I shall make a ridiculous claim. I propose that
the surest guide to sound artistic assessment is Jesus Christ;
and even as I say it I am embarrassed by anything so gauche
and crude.

I don't mean that Christians make the best critics. The two
critics in my lifetime I have read with most profit, Kenneth
Tynan and Bernard Levin, have not been Christians. I don't

mean that being a Christian gives you answers to the difficult questions. I don't mean that Christian art is best. You only have to state that to see how incredible that is. Yet I repeat: the surest guide to discerning what is best in artistic matters is Jesus Christ.

It's easier to begin with Bach or Rembrandt or Tolstoy. Few, I think, would dispute their right to be considered among the best; and none could dispute their Christianity or their explicit desire to glorify God in their work. So with the nameless architects of Amiens cathedral, where the soaring, narrow, heavenly space is designed to reflect the building of the City of God. I think it makes sense to say both the more you know Amiens cathedral the more you know God, and the more you know God the more you understand Amiens.

But this Festival is about Tchaikovsky; and Hugh Mac-Diarmid; and all sorts of other deep creative souls who cared little for Christ, or who despised Christ, or who never heard of Christ. What sense is there in saying that for them the surest guide to discerning what is best in artistic matters is Jesus Christ? Where does that leave Shelley, or primeval cave-painters, or the music of India? Is not this Christian imperialism?

In her novel *The Bell*, Iris Murdoch describes the visit of a woman called Dora to an art gallery. The significant moment there was in front of a painting by Gainsborough. It is a clear and touching account of a deep experience of art. Her memory of the experience was that 'She felt she had had a revelation'. Seeing the painting was 'something real, something perfect'; and Dora went away 'feeling favoured, encouraged, loved'. It is religious language. She felt that she had been allowed to see a deep mystery, that she had touched the secret of life itself.

The secret of life itself. Revelation. Could these be useful words for speaking about art, about the Edinburgh Festival, about Bach and Tchaikovsky, about Tolstoy and Shelley? Can you taste some moment in your own life when it might almost have been as it was for Dora in the art gallery? More than a catch in the throat; more than just excitement. But somehow true! Somehow real! Somehow perfect!

As I was thinking about Dora in the art gallery, 'favoured, encouraged and loved', I deliberately refused to check up on the life of Gainsborough. It may seem to you woeful ignorance that I confess to you that I have no idea what, if any, were Gainsborough's religious beliefs. But what better illustration could there be that it does not ultimately matter? So profound is her experience, so deep is the mystery, so powerful is the revelation that it itself is what matters, the taste of life it puts into her mouth is the artistic experience; and the artist's own beliefs fade into the background.

What art is about is the holiest and most human places in our lives; the very centre of existence itself. No wonder the words sound feeble. How could mere words capture the music of Handel we are listening to today? The holiest and most human places in our lives; the very centre of existence itself. That is what makes art matter and matter hugely; that is what the Edinburgh Festival ought to be about. And these very things are things about which Christians have something to say.

For the centre of the Christian claim is nothing less than this. Whatever is really real, whatever is the secret of life, whatever holds the universe together and makes the stars go around – that is what meets us in Jesus Christ. In Jesus Christ the creative life that has been from the beginning takes form and speaks and loves and heals and suffers. 'In the beginning was the Word and the Word was with God . . . And the Word became a human person and dwelt among us.'

It is because I believe that Jesus Christ is the secret of life that I make the claim that the surest guide to discerning what is best in artistic matters is Jesus Christ. I believe that he is the secret of life not in the sense that he is a code to give answers to those who sign up; but in the sense that the very deepest, the most real things, what it is that makes human life human, the energy and love and light of the world are to be met in him. The more we dare to know him, the more we seek to love him, the more we allow him to stay with us, the more we learn to follow, the closer, the closer will be our understanding of what really matters. As we see him more clearly, love him more dearly, follow him more nearly the better will be our feeling for what is at the heart of things, the more sure will be our knowledge of what life itself really is.

Iris Murdoch used the language of the gospel stories when she said that the woman in front of the Gainsborough painting knew herself to be 'favoured, encouraged and loved'. Jesus Christ invites us to walk with him into true humanity. How then could it not be that with him we will know better what is real, what is true, what is perfect? How could it not be that with him we will know better what is sham and thin and inadequate and second-rate? With more confidence I repeat the claim of the beginning. The surest guide to discerning what is best in artistic matters is Jesus Christ.

Eight days ago in the Usher Hall the opening concert of the Festival was Schoenberg's *Moses and Aaron*, the story of the rage of Moses as his brother builds a golden calf for Israel. That story has had a negative influence on Jewish and Protestant attitudes to the visual arts; but it cannot mean that God is against beauty: there is too much scriptural evidence to the contrary. I think the story means that God is against anything, beautiful or ugly, that gets in the way of his people's love for him and gets in the way of their knowing and receiving his love. The calf was deliberately built to take the place of God; and when anything does that – and art can do it as viciously as sex or money or pride – then that is what the Bible calls idolatry. But art can be used, as in the psalms of Israel or the stories of Jesus or the ornamentation of the Heavenly City in the book of Revelation. Used like that, or in the paintings of Gainsborough or the music of Tchaikovsky and Scott Joplin, then there is no more powerful or holy or loving way to taste the kingdom of God.

The full text from Philippians is: 'That your love may overflow more and more with knowledge and full insight, to help you determine what is best.' The best way to become an expert critic of the arts is to learn to pray. Amen.

Part 6

Preaching about current affairs

ST ANDREW, SCOTLAND AND FAMILY VALUES

(At the Annual Service for the Knights of the Thistle)

If on this day we were to speak of Scotland as the Bible encourages us, then we might speak of the family of Scotland. That is certainly a biblical way of speaking. In the passage we have read from the book of Jeremiah the family metaphor is used of Israel. In the book of Amos God says that they are the only nation he has known 'of all the families of the earth'. And so on. I invite you to follow the model of the Bible and speak of this nation as a family.

Everywhere you go these days you hear about them; and I'm very much in favour of family values. I'm delighted that they are at the forefront of the political agenda. I think every Christian minister would want to support and defend family values. Yet when I hear the stuff and nonsense which is talked in the name of family values; when I hear the narrow-mindedness and intolerance which is defended in the name of family values; when I hear the ignorance and opportunism which masquerades under the name of family values I wonder what kind of family I've been living in.

Here are some of the values I want to matter in my family. These are what I mean by family values; and they are precisely the values I want us to be famous for. One is that the big ones help the wee ones. My mother-in-law was one of thirteen children: and no one in the school playground ever dared to upset her youngest sister! It doesn't always happen: but it can be one of the most formative and valuable experiences of family life to discover that the big ones help the wee ones. I want that family value for Scotland.

Can it be true that 300,000 tiny Scots live under the poverty line? That's the number of under-fives counted as seriously poor in a report I read recently. That is one in three children. I'm not going to listen to smooth talk about 'definitions of poverty' and 'unreliability of statistics'. Go to twenty Church of Scotland parishes in this city alone; let the parish minister tell you one or two stories; and you will know that poor people really are poor; and poor children poorest of all. If it was 200,000 children in Scotland today it would be a disgrace. If it was 50,000 children in Scotland today it would be a disgrace. It is 300,000 under-fives.

Family values means the big ones help the wee ones. How proud we could be of Scotland if we went from this place resolved on that family value alone: resolved to attack, attack, attack the crime of poverty until the wee ones of the family know that they are as safe as my mother-in-law in the school playground. One family value Scotland needs is compassion.

The next of our family values must be common to almost everyone here. Last Sunday we had eighteen ministers and their husbands and wives for lunch. Unfortunately we were only at the soup when we realized that ministers on Sundays, at least, take the pleasures of the table almost as a Christian duty! Would 50 meringues be enough? So the family value everyone applies is 'family hold back' and for that purpose two couples were enrolled on the spot as honorary family so that they could hold back as well! A family value in many a home is 'family hold back'. A good family value for the family of the nation.

Recently I was at the Treasury meeting a Treasury minister. I was there in obedience to the General Assembly which instructed me to tell the government of the deep sadness in the Church of Scotland over the failure of successive governments to keep long-standing promises about overseas aid. We are committed to an agreed United Nations target for aid for the Third World. Instead of getting nearer to the target we are falling further and further behind. There are strong self-interest arguments in building healthy economies in poor countries: arguments about developing new markets and creating political stability. But beyond these there are overwhelming moral arguments: about justice and about loving your neighbour. In the face of these arguments 'family hold back' is a good family value. Sacrifice is an old-fashioned word, but I am not ashamed to use it in this context. It is an old-fashioned value we need. I long to see this nation giving a moral lead to the whole world. Another family value Scotland needs is sacrifice.

For a third family value for Scotland I want to tell you a story. It is a story about a marriage. Alan Paton wrote the beautiful novel *Cry, the Beloved Country* in 1948. It was for many people the first realization of what was going on in South Africa. He also wrote the best book about prayer I have ever read. In his autobiography he writes about falling in love with a woman and carrying on an affair with her, deceiving his wife.

Eventually his wife confronted him and Paton immediately determined to stop the affair. 'I ask only one thing', he said to his wife, 'and that is to go down to Natal and say goodbye to her.' It was a painful parting, described with great poignancy. Then the story continues: 'The day after I had said goodbye to Joan, I drove back the four hundred miles to Johannesburg, subdued and quiet. Dorrie met me at the door of the house, and took me in her arms in that strange fierce way she had when she meant something intensely, and held back her head so that I could see the earnestness in her face, and said to me, "I am going to make it all up to you".'

What would you call it? Forgiveness? Reconciliation? Whatever it is it represents something that the nation needs. A family value of acceptance, of generosity. It is perhaps the value above all that makes families work; which keeps them together. This family of Scotland will only work if we can grow in generosity of spirit, in acceptance of each other, in turning away from grudge and division, in learning to love one another. A family value of love.

Scotland as a family. Family values for the nation. Compassion and sacrifice and love.

But we're not quite done; because the Bible won't let us finish there. If you preach from a Christian pulpit about family values you need to confront the uncomfortable fact that every single New Testament reference to Jesus' own family after Bethlehem is unhappy. The misunderstanding with his parents at the Temple in the only teenage story; the evident antagonism of his brothers; the strained relationship throughout with his mother. There is enough, you would have thought, to have kept preachers away from sentimental twaddle about simple family bliss. No family is simply blissful and the Holy Family does not seem to have been so either.

Worse still, preachers on family values cannot ignore the hard sayings of Jesus about the family. We read this morning 'I have come to set a man against his father . . . and whoever loves son or daughter more than me is not worthy of me'. Could it be that all this uneasiness in the New Testament about family might be pointing to a loyalty beyond family? To a recognition that families can be wonderful and instruments of divine love; but they can also be cruel and possessive and get in the way of the things that really matter; and get in the way of God? Perhaps the Bible is afraid that family might sometimes work to turn people away from God and God's presence and God's demand and God's love.

If so, St Andrew is a hero. Not only a saint; but a hero. For the New Testament suggests that he managed to get that difficult balance right. He managed to hold together these two loyalties, both so strong. For the family values are there. Over and over it is Andrew and his brother Peter. They stick together to the end. They are together in the first story in which Andrew is mentioned; and they are together in the last. It is Andrew and his brother and family values.

But it is more than that. It is Andrew and his brother and Jesus Christ. At the start it is bringing Peter to Jesus; at the end it is going with Peter and Jesus to the Mount of Olives for the great and terrible vision of the coming of the kingdom of God. Andrew managed to find an environment of family values which didn't get in the way, but which supported and helped and nourished faith and the company of Jesus Christ and the presence and love of God. A hero for Scotland; and one in whose footsteps we might bring Scotland and its family values nearer and nearer to God. Amen.

HOMELESS

(At the Service of Dedication and Thanksgiving
for the Rock Trust)

Ten miles west of Ardgay on a minor road in Strathcarron, Sutherland, lies Croick church. There is a painful message scratched a century and a half ago on the glass of the East window. It was the end of the Highland Clearances, that terrible time in Scottish history when poor people were driven from their homes to make room for profitable sheep. The factor of Glencalvie dispossessed the last people in the glen. *The Times* reported in 1845: 'It was a most wretched spectacle to see these 88 poor people march out of the glen in a body, with two or three carts filled with children, many of them mere infants.' It was wet and cold and they made their way to the church at Croick for shelter. They found the church locked against them; but they sought some kind of shelter in the churchyard for several days. Today the pathetic message on the window can still be read: 'Glencalvie people – the wicked generation.'

I'm haunted by that scratch on the glass at Croick church. Haunted by the picture of men and women, boys and girls in the cold of Highland nights, coming in a crisis to the church for shelter: and finding the doors of the church locked in their faces. Haunted by the wicked silence of Christian people who read their Bibles every morning and every evening and said nothing when a whole generation was turned out of house and home. With the shining exception of Donald Sage of Kildonan, the wicked silence of Christian people. But of course, things are very different now.

I'm haunted by the message – 'Glencalvie people – the

107

wicked generation' – because I know what it means. These miserable people had been taught that their pitiable story was their punishment. They were being turned out of house and home because they had been lazy and unprofitable. They were homeless because they were wicked. What a vile deceit it is – and how pervasive it is – to assert that the victims of cruelty and injustice are to blame – to blame themselves! – for their own misfortunes. Did I say that things were different nowadays?

Last week an Albanian doctor was staying with us. As we walked together around the centre of this wonderful city how could we speak of Edinburgh's young homeless? Coming from a country of fearful poverty where two rooms is a luxury house, how could I make him understand why people in Britain slept in the graveyards of our churches? Ashamed, embarrassed, and confused, I knew that the easiest thing to do is to find someone to blame.

So I blamed the government, and I still do. The Citizen's Charter and the classless society are a joke if you don't have a roof over your head. I blamed the local authority, and I still do. No doubt they do their best; but their best is not good enough. I blamed society: how can you explain to someone who has lived all his life under tyranny that democracy means the freedom to live in poverty and squalor? I blamed the churches, and I still do. There was a day when the churches were the conscience of the nation, but now it is not decent to give offence. I blamed myself, and I still do. Miserable as it is to admit it, I have learned to adjust to the pain that is daily before my eyes. You can always find some-one to blame; and there will usually be those who think the best people to blame are the victims themselves.

Still the Albanian did not understand. Then I told him about the Rock Trust. I began to speak of the remarkable achievement of a few short months in doing something about homelessness in Edinburgh. I told him that this was an adventure in hope; and it reminded me of other adven-tures in hope which refuse to walk away from Edinburgh's homeless. Different people doing different kinds of things;

but all of them thinking that there are better things to do than blame people. Hoping is better than blaming. Hoping is always better than blaming. As we spoke about houses made ready and breakfasts served and money gathered and prayers said it all became more human, more possible.

In the story of the Good Samaritan the side of the road is crowded with people passing by and blaming. It is lonely out in the middle of the road healing the wounds. But it is the Samaritan who holds the future in his hands, not those who pass by. The Samaritan is a figure of hope; and hoping is always better than blaming. The way we treat homeless people in Scotland is a disgrace; a disgrace to government, a disgrace to local authorities, a disgrace to society, a disgrace to individual consciences, a disgrace to the churches. But let the Good Samaritan transform blame and shame into hope and determination. Let the Rock Trust open a door to a future where homelessness is no longer tolerated or accepted or even known among us. A future where a safe and dry and healthy house is for everyone and none is left outside in the cold. A future where God's will is done, where his justice reigns, and none is too poor, too ill, too inadequate, nor too neglected to share.

Recently I was speaking at a Housing Coalition meeting on the anniversary of the thanksgiving service for the life of George MacLeod. I told then his story of the founding of the Iona Community. In the thirties George MacLeod was preaching on the streets of Govan when a man in the crowd shouted 'Do you think all this religious stuff will save?' George asked him to come up on the platform, but he refused and left the meeting. A few weeks later the minister of Govan was called to hospital to see a man called Archie Gray. When George MacLeod reached the hospital he discovered that Archie Gray was the man in the crowd and he was dying of starvation. He said he was bitter about the church, not because it was preaching falsehoods, but because it was speaking the truth and did not mean what it said.

George MacLeod always said that Archie Gray was the true founder of the Iona Community. He said he was bitter about the church, not because it was preaching falsehoods, but because it was speaking the truth and did not mean what it said.

The truth is written in the prophet Isaiah. 'The fruit of righteousness will be peace; the effect of righteousness will be quietness and confidence for ever. My people will live in peaceful dwelling-places, in secure homes, in undisturbed places of rest.' The Rock Trust helps us all to speak the truth, and to mean what we say.

Amen.

RACIAL JUSTICE

The Letter to Philemon

The worst thing about being a slave was that they took your name away. They gave you a pet name, as you would give to a dog. To make it clear who was boss. They took away your name, your family, your inheritance. They gave you a slave name. You were owned. That is what lay behind the much misunderstood gesture of the great boxer, Cassius Clay. When he took the name of Muhammad Ali, in part it was refusing to carry a slave name any longer.

They gave you a pet name. Like 'useful', for example. Onesimus in the Greek. That was a cracker – it always made them laugh: 'useful by name and useful by nature.' That one always got a chuckle. They gave you a name, like a dog. That was the worst thing about being a slave.

No it wasn't. The worst thing about being a slave was the cruelty. The slave was continually at the caprice of master or mistress. The Roman law stated: 'The owner may punish them with blows of the rod, the lash or the knot; he can brand them upon the forehead, or, if they prove difficult, he can crucify them.' The Roman writer Pliny describes the treatment of one slave: 'he was carrying a tray of crystal goblets into the courtyard; he dropped one and broke it; on the instant his owner ordered the slave to be thrown into the fishpond in the middle of the court, where they watched him being torn to pieces by the savage lampreys.' Slavery was hell.

Ten or twenty years ago there was a television series based on an American book called *Roots*. It was the story of a slave, brought from the West Coast of Africa to America to work the farms in the hot sun. The television series did not quite have the stomach for the nauseating scenes of cruelty and outrage and sexual exploitation and sadism which peppered the book, but for all that it seared the conscience of viewers, British and American alike. It was on ships flying the Union Jack that these human cargoes were dragged in unbelievably foul conditions across the Atlantic to make white men rich. On ships crewed by Christians.

The American revivalist preacher C. G. Finney swallowed hard, and took a deep breath. He knew well enough that he was walking out of polite society. But he took a deep breath and spoke. 'The church which does not condemn slavery has perjured itself, and the Holy Spirit has departed from it.' No wonder they drove him out of the Presbyterian Church. The story of the church and slavery makes sorry reading. It is true that the most honourable names in the abolitionist movements on both sides of the Atlantic belong to Christians; but it is also true that the most powerful resistance to abolition gained its force from the blessing slavery tacitly received from the institutional churches.

This is Racial Justice Sunday. It is always easier to see the vileness of racism in other people: in Nazis or Boers or Serbs or the Ku Klux Klan. Or the people of the eighteenth century. But if we are honest, we can find things inside ourselves that shock us and shame us. It is a sobering thought that the wealth and prosperity of the developed world, which exploded in the eighteenth and nineteenth centuries, was built on the cruelty and exploitation of slavery, which recognized those of a different colour as less than human. We're part of that, however little we like it. And on this Sunday at least let us resolve that the huge injustices done by the forces of history against the black and brown peoples of the world will find no echo, no support, no encouragement, no reproduction, no continuance in our hearts, in our churches, in our country. We could all do with a little less prejudice, and a little more repentance.

Onesimus, that was one slave's name. 'Useful' is how it is

translated into English. 'Useful by name and useful by nature.' He must have really loved that one! He appears in the Bible. He is one of the key figures in the shortest surviving letter written by St Paul. We heard the whole of the letter to Philemon this morning. It is about a slave, a slave-owner and St Paul. It is an ambiguous letter. For it does not roundly condemn slavery and that has been a source of concern to readers ever since. Indeed, the whole New Testament seems to have a fairly ambiguous attitude to slavery, which today looks unfortunate. Who knows how moral our social judgements will look in two thousand years?

However, it is a fascinating letter, a 'gem of a letter', as Dr Mary Levison calls it. It is nearly possible to piece together the story which lies behind the letter, though there is enough doubt to make sure that there are alternative theories. But reading between the lines – remember that we have no source of explanation of what lies behind the letter other than what it says itself – gives a background like this.

Philemon was a prominent Christian, probably a member of the church at Colossae. He was the owner of the slave Onesimus. This slave had run away from his master, and somehow had come in contact with Paul, who was then in prison. Through Paul, Onesimus became a Christian. Then Paul writes this letter to Philemon. In the letter he appeals to the owner to be reconciled to Onesimus, whom Paul is sending back to him. Paul hopes that Philemon will welcome him not only as a forgiven slave but as a Christian brother.

Dr Levison writes this about the thinking behind this letter: 'Paul rejects the categories into which we normally divide people: rich and poor, Jew and Gentile (or black and white), slave and free. And this is not just in theory but in practice. This triangle – Paul, Philemon, and Onesimus – is an example in life of what Paul writes – that they are all one in Christ Jesus. So that, in Christ, the appropriate terms are *father and son, sister and brother, dear friend and colleague*. And these terms are appropriate across all barriers and frontiers.'

Racial justice is a concern for the churches not because of theories about society. It is because of what we believe about Jesus Christ.

After this letter Paul was released from prison. He went on to heroic missionary endeavour and to write some of the key documents of Christian faith. Philemon is never heard of again. And Onesimus? He crops up again in the Letter to the Colossians, where Paul describes him as 'faithful and beloved brother'. Apart from that . . .

Well, it is an outside chance, but listen to this. Fifty years later Ignatius, one of the great Christian martyrs, is being taken to be executed in Rome. As he goes, he writes letters to various churches. In his letter to the church at Ephesus, a letter which still survives, he has much to say about their wonderful bishop. And what is this bishop's name? It is Onesimus! Could it be that Onesimus the runaway slave became the great bishop of Ephesus? Could it be that Paul's letter to Philemon did the trick?

Amen.

HUMAN RIGHTS

He shall not judge by what his eyes see, or decide by what his ears hear.

ISAIAH 11.3

The American novelist John Grisham has a story about a murder in the Deep South. Sam Cayhall, a member of the Ku Klux Klan, has just murdered a black man called Joe Lincoln. Sam's daughter describes the arrival of the sheriff on the scene: "'He and Sam talked for a bit. Sam showed him Joe's shotgun and explained how it was a simple matter of self-defence. Just another dead nigger." "He wasn't arrested?" asked her nephew. "No Adam. This was Mississippi in the early fifties. I'm sure the sheriff had a good laugh about it, patted Sam on the back, and told him to be a good boy, and then left. He even allowed Sam to keep Joe's shotgun.'"

The most devastating expression of racism in the Deep South in the fifties was that black people did not hope for justice from the courts. The most devastating expression of racism in de Klerk's South Africa was that black people could not hope for justice from the courts. Perhaps the most interesting thing about the O. J. Simpson trial was that most white people, both in America and in Britain, thought he should be convicted and most black people, both in America and in Britain, thought he should be acquitted. The explanations of that curious fact are various and deep: but at least they suggest that there are huge problems for a legal system when large numbers of the community assume that it is arrayed against them instead of for them.

So on Human Rights Sunday I begin with the central place of the justice system in defending freedom. One of the absolutely defining marks of civilization, of decent society, is

115

that every member of the community – whatever the appearance, whatever the rumours – can expect a fair hearing. Wherever there is the faintest touch of corruption or bias or special interest in the courts, it is the weak and the poor who suffer most. You can understand in ancient Israel, under the violent and corrupt rule of Tiglath-Pileser III, King of Assyria, that the small people would long for the day when they could be confident of a fair hearing before a judge. So part of Isaiah's promise of the coming Messiah is 'He will not judge by outward appearances or decide a case on hearsay'.

Last week at St Giles' Cathedral there was a memorial service for a great man, Sir Francis Akanu Ibiam. Academic, doctor, politician, king, President of the World Council of Churches, he may have been the only Church of Scotland missionary ever to get a trial for Glasgow Rangers! But what made this service so poignant was that Sir Francis Akanu Ibiam was a Nigerian. So woven into this service of thanksgiving was the horror and the fear and the pain of so many people over what is happening in Nigeria today. I've been involved a little in trying to frame church responses to the execution of Ken Saro-Wiwa: and one of the three things for which the Church and Nation Committee is pressing (hand in hand with the British Government) is that the independence of the courts be restored. The nastiest thing about the nasty business of Ken Saro-Wiwa was the iron fist of the General holding the judges' arms up their backs.

Salamat Masih made world headlines recently. He was a fourteen-year-old boy who had been sentenced to death in Pakistan for blasphemy. All sorts of people, again including the Church of Scotland, were concerned at the time that malicious charges had been brought and he had not received a fair trial. Salamat was later acquitted of the charge. His lawyer wrote to us and many others on his behalf when he was in prison, expressing his thanks for the thousands of letters which kept his head above water. Again, the central issue here was the judicial system, and the determination of the government to make sure that the courts did as they were told and saw the world in the way they were told.

'He shall not judge by what his eyes see, or decide by what his ears hear.' You would be quite wrong to think that this is all politics and no Bible. It is one of the many places where politics and the Bible walk hand in hand. It is the Bible which emphasizes a fair trial as one of the signs of God's kingdom. It is the Bible which calls us to care about injustice everywhere. For injustice anywhere is injustice everywhere.

Of course it is comforting to us to listen to these attacks on the USA and Nigeria and Pakistan. We know that we have the best courts you can have, and the best judges you can have. I actually believe that to be true; but I am also sure that all of us, not just judges, not just MPs, need to cherish our system of justice, need to listen to criticisms of it, need to be aware of how it looks to all sections of our community and not just to prosperous white people, and need to pray for judges.

'He shall not judge by what his eyes see, or decide by what his ears hear.' Which is wonderful if you are oppressed or discriminated against or victimized. But what about the rest of us? Is this bit of Bible, this Advent hope, this Christmas good news, anything for us? Why should I want to hear that God will judge fairly? Why should I want to hear that God will judge at all?

To tell the truth, most of the time I don't want to hear that! But it is part of the Christian message, and it is particularly and traditionally part of the Advent message. God coming as judge. Christians who take that seriously – and I'm not sure that you can be a Christian if you don't take it seriously – react in one of two ways to that idea.

First there are those who face God the coming judge with fear and despair. They are those who know that they are, in the old words, 'wicked and unprofitable servants'; who know that when the eyes of the just judge are turned on them they will tremble and be right to tremble. They are those who know that even their best acts are tainted with mixed motives and that secretly, deep down, they put themselves first every single time, whatever the world says about their selflessness and care for others. These are they who know that their prayers are shallow, their love for neighbour extremely conditional and their trust in God merely prudential. They are those who know that God is a jealous God, loving the right and hating the wrong, who desires mercy, not sacrifice and whose will will be done.

And to that extent I hope that you are among them.

Yet I hope you do not fear the judgement of God. For there is something else.

The second group are those who know the depth of their own sin, but also know the depth of the love of God and the sacrifice of the cross. Christian faith at its best understands the judgement of the Messiah like this. Christ, coming to us as judge sees us with terrible clarity and sees us whole. Christ's love so wishes our joy that it is ruthless against everything in us that diminishes our joy. The one who judges us most finally will be the one who loves us most fully. The worst sentence Love can pass is that we behold the suffering which Love has endured for our sake: and that is also our acquittal. The justice and the mercy of this judge are ultimately one.

Come, thou long-expected Jesus
Born to set thy people free;
From our fears and sins release us;
Let us find our rest in thee.

Amen.

A HARVEST FOR BOSNIA

(Preached in connection with Edinburgh Direct Aid,
which has roots in St Andrew's and St George's)

Flour and oil and salt could link us with the Bible on the
one hand and with former Yugoslavia on the other. With
the Bible because the kind of baking which could be done
would be very little different from the baking done outside
Abraham's tent and in any Nazareth home. With former
Yugoslavia because it will also be very little different from the
baking which will be done there in a few weeks' time with
the flour and oil and salt we have brought to church to offer
to God for the good of that bloody land. Maybe they will
have some milk, or a couple of eggs, or perhaps some sugar.
It might be bread somewhere, scones somewhere else. But it
will be flour, oil, and salt.

We brought flour and oil and salt because that is what
Edinburgh Direct Aid asked for: because that is what they
put in what they call 'Family Parcels'. But they could not
have asked for any kind of food more meaningful for the
Bible. The absolutely standard offering brought before God
– not lambs, not doves, not bulls, but flour and oil. The
proverbial sign of God's goodness from that Elijah story we
read – flour and oil. But not just flour and oil. It says in the
book of Leviticus that whenever you bring your offering of
flour and oil, you are to mix with it a little salt. Edinburgh
Direct Aid could not have asked for any food more meaningful for the Bible. Nor could they have asked for any kind
of food which would have spelt out more clearly the needs
of Bosnia, the needs of all former Yugoslavia.

No wonder they asked for flour. Grain, corn, meal, flour:

119

in my Bible dictionary they are all listed together. The article begins with an interesting sentence which gives the clue to the importance of flour here today. 'This is the all-important commodity of the Ancient East: the price of grain is an infallible index to economic conditions at any given time.' Economic conditions: flour was a symbol of that in Bible times and a symbol of that today. We don't hear as much as we should in our churches about economics. Church people are as likely as anyone else to laugh at the complexities of economics and the opportunities for disagreement which that science offers. But they should not. They should not because Jesus spoke so often in economic terms; and we should not because economics is so vastly important for the way we order society. What kind of church have we become, what kind of God do we believe in, if we allow ourselves to think that economics does not matter to God? Listen to these words from a famous economist, A. C. Pigou:

> The complicated analyses which economists attempt to carry through are not mere gymnastics. They are instruments for the bettering of human life. The misery and squalor that surround us, the injurious luxury of some wealthy families, the terrible uncertainty overshadowing many families of the poor – these are evils too plain to be ignored. By the knowledge that our science seeks it is possible that they may be restrained. Out of the darkness light! The search for it is the task, perhaps to find it the prize, which the 'dismal science of political economy' offers to those who face its discipline.

Learn to pray for economists, to think about economic systems, and to believe that economic systems, as much as sexual morality and artistic endeavour, come under the providence and judgement of God. As you bring up your flour, symbol of the economic circumstances of Bible times, hold the world of economics before God. And think of former Yugoslavia. For whatever else will be needed there if the war ever ends, what will certainly be needed is a new economy, an economic rebirth, a miraculous new start. The connections between war and economic instability and poverty are too horribly familiar all over the world. Was it not wonderful to see our Prime Minister, Mr Major, in South Africa? To see him embracing Mr Mandela and planning with him the new relationship between these two historic partners? This was much more than the healing of deep wounds. It was the beginning of the economic regeneration of South Africa which is essential, simply essential, for the future of peace and freedom so recently won there. And as in South Africa, so in former Yugoslavia. Our flour is a symbol of our yearning for the future of those lands where there is the kind of economy which can begin to repair the destruction of these last years.

No wonder Edinburgh Direct Aid asked next for oil. Back to my Bible dictionary. 'Oil was prominent among the first-fruit offerings, frequently mixed with flour. It was widely used in the preparation of food and in fuel for lamps. As a medicine it was used externally and internally.' Of all these different uses the symbol for us this morning is oil as medicine. On one level that reminds us of the particular mission Edinburgh Direct Aid has had in taking medicines to Sarajevo. Do you remember that moving story my wife told here last month? With 3,000 other women she listened to a woman from Bosnia tell for a whole hour the most harrowing stories of violence against young children in Sarajevo. At the end Irene, like most others, was in tears and felt that she had to speak to this woman. She said 'I'm Irene McLellan from Scotland'. No response. She went on, 'I come from the capital city, Edinburgh'. Immediately the woman from Sarajevo replied 'I don't know much about Scotland, but I do know Edinburgh. For there is a group called Edinburgh called Edinburgh Direct Aid. They bring medicines to our hospital in Sarajevo.'

But also oil here this morning as a symbol of healing. So that we may bring the healing of former Yugoslavia before God as we bring up our oil. Healing for Bosnia! The bodies; the minds; the spirit of the people. Healing for Croatia, for Serbia. The bodies, the minds, the spirits. Healing for the nations. Most of us find it easy, in theory at least, to believe that healing matters to God. But only in theory. The American writer Agnes Sanford has a vivid picture of Jesus standing in church services all over Christendom with his hands tied behind his back. He is unable to do any mighty works there because the ministers who lead the services either don't expect him to or don't dare ask him to for fear that he won't or can't and that their own faith and the faith of their congregations will be threatened as a result.

As you bring up your oil, think of healing. Of health services and health service workers, of people ill and in pain; of those you love who need healing. Think of Jesus the healer. And remember Bosnia.

And no wonder they asked for salt. Back to my Bible dictionary. Did you know that in Bible times newborn infants were rubbed with salt? But it's not that! Did you know that in Bible times salt was used for ratifying agreements, so it became a symbol of constancy? It might have been that this morning as we think of the people of the Balkans; but it is not. It is the most obvious biblical image: the one picked up in our gospel reading this morning. Salt as a symbol of the church. 'You are the salt of the earth': the words of Jesus to his followers.

The Bible tells us that God loves the church; and that God judges the church. What must God make of the church in former Yugoslavia? That church God loves, and that church God judges. What do you make of the church in former Yugoslavia? Or rather the churches: for one of the deadly things about this conflict is the analysis which suggest that there are hints of a Christian war against Islam; and of a war between Orthodoxy and Catholicism.

It is more than a year now since I was there; but I remember crying with a minister of a tiny Reformed congregation, in danger of his freedom and his life, when he told me that his message every Sunday was 'Love your enemies'. I remember crying in a different spirit after meeting the Orthodox Patriarch in Belgrade and the Catholic Cardinal in Zagreb: for I thought then and I think still that neither of them was prepared or equipped to lead their church out of the role of puppet or prisoner of the state: a role in which the churches were manipulated to give some legitimacy, some sanctification, to the most naked aggression. When from time to time people indicate to me that it is the task of the Church and Nation Committee to give uncritical loyal support to the government I remember Yugoslavia and shudder.

This salt is a symbol of the church. The church in former Yugoslavia. The church in Scotland. St Andrew's and St George's. The church which is loved by God and judged by God. As you pray for that church, will you remember that you are praying for yourself?

Amen.

Part 7
Preaching about places

GENEVA

(Preached on the Fiftieth Anniversary of the United Nations
in The Scots' Kirk, Geneva)

Wise people celebrate the United Nations and pray for its health and vigour. Wise people. And that is a statement of theology.

A statement of theology that was born in this very building. I say wise people wish the United Nations well because of what John Calvin said in this very building, when he began his lectures on the Institutes of the Christian Religion with this sentence: 'Our wisdom consists almost entirely of two parts: our knowledge of God and of ourselves.' Because of what we know about God and because of what we know about ourselves, rightly today we salute the United Nations.

A beginning which sounds as if it comes from another planet. I mean to say, who in their right minds can muster three cheers for the United Nations these days? Whisper to me Somalia, whisper to me Bosnia, whisper to me the hunger of the world's poor, and surely I will say that only a fool can celebrate the United Nations. Wrong! I say wise people give thanks today: because of what we know about God, and what we know about ourselves.

I know that God cares about history. All of the Old Testament is the story of wars and alliances and power and deliverances and slavery and treaties and politics. That's what you get in Exodus, that's what you get in First Kings, that's what you get in Jeremiah. In the great religions of the East the divine force is found in contemplation or in self-denial or in insight: the God of the Bible is found in history, in what happens to people. In the rescuing of a whole nation from the bonds of Egyptian slavery; in the exile of that same people in Babylon. In the birth of a baby in the year there went out a decree from Caesar Augustus that all the world should be taxed, in that baby's execution under Pontius Pilate. In all these historical events the Bible tells us to look for God: it is in these historical events that God is to be found. It is in the history of the twentieth century that twentieth-century people are to look for God. The God of the Bible cares about what happens to people.

Second, I know God cares about peace. I know it from the great prophetic passages in Isaiah: 'He shall judge between the nations, and shall arbitrate for many peoples: and they shall beat their swords into ploughshares, and their spears into pruninghooks: nation shall not lift up sword against nation, neither shall they learn war any more.' I know it from the words of Jesus who promised that it is the peacemakers who will be called the children of God. I know it from the cross of Jesus who died that we might be reconciled to each other and to God.

Third, what I know of God is unremitting, relentless concern for the weak and the defenceless and the vulnerable. There was once a student for the ministry who decided to go right through his Bible cutting out every single reference to the poor. It took him a very long time. The Old Testament, the prophets, the Psalms, the law – all decimated. In the New Testament so many of the words of Jesus, the book of Acts, the letter of James, the letters of John – snip, snip, snip. When the student was finished, that old Bible hung in threads. It wouldn't hold together It was a Bible full of holes. And then that student would take that holey old Bible with him to preach. He would hold it high above American congregations – for he was an American – and he would say 'Friends, this is the American Bible, full of holes from all that we have cut out'. So in America, so in Scotland, so through-out the rich North and West. We just cut out all the bits we don't want to hear about the poor, the weak, the vulnerable. And the result is a Bible so full of holes that it falls apart in our hands.

When Calvin said that true wisdom is what we know of God, what I know of God is about history and about peace and about the poor. Which is exactly what the United Nations is about. Its problems are on everyone's lips these days. I could wish its great ideals could be in everyone's hearts. The ideals of its preamble, of a world free from war and overcoming poverty. The very ideals of the Christian God.

The second part of wisdom, said Calvin, is the knowledge of ourselves. Again, because of what I know about human beings, I am a passionate advocate of the United Nations. What I know about ourselves is what I know from the Bible and from Jesus Christ. I know two things about human beings, and because of both of them I am glad to celebrate the United Nations and pray for its future.

The first thing I know about ourselves is that we are sinners. Calvin has had a bad press for centuries, but on this he was absolutely right and history has proved it so no more shockingly than in this century and on this continent. We are all sinners: there is in every one of us a tendency to screw things up and to choose what is hurtful and to turn our backs on God. There is in the whole human race a poisoned bit that will always prefer darkness to light. A compulsion to reverse the brave words written on the Reformation Wall here in Geneva to read *Post lucem tenebrae* – 'after light the darkness'.

It was absolutely right that I should be taken immediately on my arrival in this city to visit the Red Cross Museum. If you have never been in Geneva you arrive starry-eyed about history and international institutions of church and state and the Alps. But it is essential, if you are to understand Geneva, to place that history and these international institutions in the context of the Red Cross Museum. In the context of the battle of Solferino and the tablets round the walls for each and every year of war and disaster and the rows and rows and rows of cards for these innumerable prisoners of war.

I'll never be persuaded that we should just leave each nation to get on with its own affairs; that we're better without any attempts at control or agreement or coming together. Even if the story of this century had not taught us what happens if we just leave the nations of the world to sort things out as best suits their own interests, Christian theology makes it clear that if nations, just like individuals, are simply left to protect their own interests they will always seek to do it in a way that will damage the interests of others. Because every nation has sinful tendencies in it, we need, we need, the United Nations.

The second thing I know about ourselves, and I know it from the Bible and from Jesus Christ, is that we belong together. We belong together. Human beings were made for each other. Cut off and apart and separated and individualized we are less than we might be. The goal of life is the city of God where we will all live together in community. In the first chapter of the Bible the man and the woman are given to each other for they were made for each other. In the last chapters of the Bible men and women come together from every nation and every race, in numbers more than can be counted, to walk in the streets of the city of God and shelter under the tree whose leaves are for the healing of the nations. We were made for each other. Jesus Christ died to bring together those who are far off and those who are near, to break down the wall of enmity between them. And that is the glorious possibility of the United Nations, the most ambitious attempt ever to put into practice, into structural form, the classical Christian virtue of loving your neighbour. The world cannot do without the United Nations, it cannot do without that precious vision of a world in which we all belong together. Let the United Nations die, and something uniquely precious about human beings, created by God for each other, dies with it.

An Indian Guru asked his disciples how they could tell when the night had ended and the day had begun. One said 'When you see an animal in the distance and can tell whether it is a cow or a horse'. 'No', said the Guru. 'When you look at a tree in the distance and can tell if it is a neem tree or a mango tree.' 'Wrong again', said the Guru. 'Well, then, what is it?' asked his disciples. 'When you look into the face of any man and recognize your brother in him; when you look into the face of any woman and recognize in her your sister. If you cannot do this, no matter what time it is by the sun it is still night.'

Amen.

THE TRANSFIGURATION OF EUROPE

LUKE 9.28–36

To keep together the part of my life which is St Andrew's and St George's and the part which is the Church and Nation Committee is difficult. But when it works naturally it makes me happy. Like the beginning and ending of my visit to the European Political Institutions. The Moderator was making an official visit to the Parliament and to NATO and he wanted me with him to deal with matters within the interest of the Church and Nation Committee. So it sounds like a completely General Assembly week. Except that our very first meeting was in the offices of the European Parliament in Strasbourg and when I walked in to this particular room there was a photograph of a young member of St Andrew's and St George's who used to work there: I clapped my hands with delight. On Sunday at church in Brussels someone asked where I worked. The response to my answer was 'Oh, the Christian Aid church'. And at almost our last meeting, with the British Ambassador to the European Union, himself a Scot, I heard him say 'I suppose the most influential Scot in Europe at the moment is . . .' and then he named another member of St Andrew's and St George's! So at the beginning, in the middle and at the end of a Church and Nation week I was full of thoughts of St Andrew's and St George's.

On Sunday, as I said, I went to church. It was St Andrew's in Brussels – the local Church of Scotland congregation. The Moderator preached on that great psalm we read this morning. 'As a deer longs for flowing streams, so my soul

131

longs for you, O God. My soul thirsts for God, for the living God.' It's one of the psalms which scholars feel may have been written by a woman. He was preaching on the yearning, the deep seeking, for God which even the most irreligious sometimes feel; and he began with Cleopatra's famous line in Shakespeare's play, just before her death: 'Give me my robe, put on my crown; I have immortal longings in me.' And I couldn't get the psalm out of my head, and I couldn't get the yearning out of my head, and I couldn't get Cleopatra out of my head. Wherever I went, I seemed to be in touch with 'immortal longings'. That's not just the individual soul. I think that is Europe itself.

I felt the longings of Europe very strongly at the European Union, at the political institutions, at the Parliament and the Commission. You probably know, but I needed to be reminded, that the whole thing was Winston Churchill's dream. A high-ranking official, a German, was able to give us the exact date in Churchill's diary – sometime in 1940, mark that date! – when he first set out his vision of a new Europe, united by common ties and a common commitment to peace and a common determination that war would never again lacerate the continent. So short is our historical memory that we forget all too quickly that deep craving for peace, that immortal longing, in which the Union was born. In time Churchill and Ernest Bevin both had to drop the idea because of pressure from Moscow and Washington; but when Robert Schuman and Konrad Adenauer took the first steps to making common cause in the fifties it was not simply out of the economic interest of iron and steel, though that was where they began. It was with a passionate idealism – indeed a specifically Christian idealism – which understood that the only way to be sure that people do not keep killing each other is by learning to live together. We do well to remember the colossal success of that founding principle: a success which means that it is now unthinkable that France and Germany would go to war against each other – those historic enemies whose antagonism has shed the blood of how many millions over how many centuries?

'I have immortal longings in me.' When I heard again the story of that early vision something deep stirred in me. Something which longs still to build a better world, which thinks it not silly to talk of vision and dreams and principles in political life. Something which is crushed when the concept of Europe becomes simply talk about common currency and the Common Agricultural Policy. Something which reminded me of the plea from the last President of the European Commission that we must find 'the soul of Europe'. Something which heard the words of the Bible about how impossible it is to talk of loving God whom we have not seen if we cannot love those we live right beside. A longing – yes, an immortal longing – to live together with my neighbour. To go beyond party politics to something deeper, to something spiritual. A soul for Europe.

Just as strongly I felt 'immortal longings' at the head-quarters of NATO. This was the first visit ever by any Moderator of the General Assembly to Britain's most important military commitment. We had long private meetings with the diplomat who heads our political delegation there, and the Air Marshal who heads our military team, both of them Christians. We met the top American Admiral, and German diplomats and British civil servant and a Turk. We talked about war and peace, about Russia and Bosnia. We talked about the Church of Scotland and the positions of the General Assembly. We talked about nuclear weapons and chemical weapons and biological weapons. We talked about training soldiers for peace-making and about money and about NATO. We talked about our own government and our own soldiers. And I felt 'immortal longings'. Longings for peace.

By coincidence the journalist Joyce Macmillan also paid her first visit to NATO last month, and for once I did not agree completely with her. I did agree with her that there is something particularly male about the world of top military diplomacy, and that that must be dangerous for us all. But I felt more strongly than she did real longings for peace in that military alliance. Before I went I assumed I would find an alliance in disarray as it searched in vain for a new enemy to take the place of the great Soviet bear. Looking for someone else to be against. And that is what Joyce Macmillan did find. To be sure, that was around; but I am convinced that it was not the driving force. The driving force was a longing for peace. I agree with her that soldiers and diplomats don't always see quite the same picture that others see; and that their strategies may not always be the ones most likely to lead to peace. But about the longing for peace I am in no doubt. We need to feel that ourselves. That longing for peace. Just as we need to get beyond economics to a soul for Europe, so we need to get beyond tactics to a soul for NATO. All the people we met there were so grateful that the Church of Scotland had met them and listened to them. Because they need help, spiritual help, to translate that longing for peace into policies that build peace.

Another visitor to Belgium last week was a Finnish Archbishop. He gave a lecture in which he argued that the place for the churches to find the soul of Europe is not in Brussels but in Helsinki and in Edinburgh. It is at home we must find the soul of Europe. So the churches can only offer that help to those who are longing for peace at NATO when we too commit ourselves to that longing for peace. To be ourselves peace-builders and peacemakers. To seek to build peace in our own lives, in our congregation, in our nation, in the North Atlantic and in the world. It is far too important to be left to people in Brussels. Peace is an immortal longing of us all.

I called this sermon 'The transfiguration of Europe'. On the mountain-top with Jesus his closest friends, those who loved him most, saw beyond what everyone else saw to a new, spiritual, dazzling reality. For a moment they saw his glory. I pray that we may nourish these immortal longings in Europe until we see through the institutions everyone else sees, see beyond all the difficulties and rows and self-interest and greed, see deep into what might yet be, until we see a soul, a spiritual reality, a real community, until we learn to live together in peace.

For there is a hole in the heart of Europe today; and that disability can only be cured by a rebirth of the spirit.

Amen.

SOUTH AFRICA

I am the good shepherd
JOHN 10.11
(Before the elections in South Africa)

There is a lovely road that runs from Ixopo into the hills. These hills are grass-covered and rolling, and they are lovely beyond any singing of it . . . The grass is rich and matted, you cannot see the soil . . . Stand unshod upon it for the ground is holy, being even as it came from the Creator. Keep it, guard it, care for it.

Do you recognize it? On this Sunday when we read of Jesus, the Good Shepherd, it must be a book about a shepherd. Well, the Latin word for 'shepherd' is *pastor*; and this is the opening of a famous book about a minister. For so many people in Europe and America, their first hint of what South Africa was becoming was Alan Paton's 1948 book *Cry, the Beloved Country*. The Rev. Stephen Kumalo discovers that his son has murdered the son of a white farmer, James Jarvis. When Absalom Kumalo is condemned to death, his father takes responsibility for his pregnant wife. The novel ends with the reconciliation of Jarvis and Kumalo, and Jarvis's determination to rise above tragedy by helping the poor black community. This moving book is about Stephen Kumalo, about what family means, about racism and understanding; but most of all it is about South Africa.

So will this sermon be. For 25 years South Africa has been in my sermons; and seldom have I mentioned that sad and lovely land without annoying some people. I do not for a moment regret anything I have said in the last 25 years to denounce tyranny and to defend freedom; but today it is going to be different. Today, for the first time in my life, it may be possible to preach about South Africa and unite us all. A friend of mine returned from two months there last week and gave me a little badge. It is the badge they are wearing in these last days before the elections – a badge which stands for peace. The fine thing is that they are all wearing it: black radicals and Boer farmers. I was wearing it proudly the other day when a shopkeeper asked me what it meant. I told him it was for peace and fair elections in South Africa: whereupon he hugged me and gave me my cheese for nothing!

So first could we agree, all of us, about the importance of peace and fair elections in South Africa? None of us could have predicted, five years ago, that next Thursday South Africa would become a democratic country. None of us know what the next five days will bring; nor what the next five months will bring. But not even an ostrich would say it doesn't matter. It matters for all Africa; for the fate of so much of Africa is tied in so many ways to what happens south of the Limpopo. It matters for all the world: for the eyes of the whole world are certainly upon South Africa this week; and the hearts of so many, including millions and millions who like me have never been there, are missing beats. It matters supremely for South Africa itself. I think perhaps only those who have never been allowed to vote know how deeply, deeply it matters.

There are vigils all over the country this week, simple witnesses that next Thursday really matters. So would you, sometime today, on your way home from church or on your Sunday afternoon walk, spend a few minutes at St John's Church as a simple witness that next Thursday really matters? These are not demonstrations; they are not just for political activists. They are for everyone who cares about democracy and freedom, and wants that precious gift to be shared wider still and wider.

Could we next agree that the word for South Africa must be *reconciliation*? I've hinted already that I hope that this turning point in South Africa will be an opportunity for reconciliation here in Scotland. There is no doubt that South African questions have divided British people deeply; and until the change began four years ago it was increasingly difficult to talk to others across the divide. Now all of us can come together in a common hope for the future of that land. If we cannot manage reconciliation here, what right have we to expect it of those there for whom reconciliation must be much more difficult?

But reconciliation there there must be. It has been the theme of Nelson Mandela's campaign; it has been supported by F. W. de Klerk; and it has been strikingly demonstrated in the *rapprochement* between these two and Chief Buthelezi in the last few days. The difficulties of reconciliation in South Africa are huge; but they *must* be faced. Here are two stories. My friend who gave me the badge has been in South Africa for two months as a World Council of Churches Peace Monitor. She returned enormously hopeful. Hopeful of fair elections, hopeful of peace, hopeful – and she is no fool – of economic recovery. But the problems are huge. People *are* being killed; people *do* have unrealistic hopes; people *are* afraid. She told me about driving down a magnificent, sparkling, tree-lined motorway until she reached the entry to a township of quarter of a million people. 'Welcome to Etwatwa' said the sign – and everything stopped! The motorway stopped, the trees stopped, the flowers stopped, and the litter lay uncollected by the side of the track. Most of us can only guess what reconciliation must mean in South Africa.

The other story is about Wilhelm Verwoerd. He is the grandson of Hendrik Verwoerd, Prime Minister of South Africa in the fifties and one of the architects of apartheid. For him the turning point came when he met Mandela, who had been jailed by his grandfather. 'The first thing he did was to ask after the health of my grandmother, who is 92. It was a genuine concern, not a political gesture. I was deeply moved, as were the people around me. I only wanted to say one thing to him, which I did. "I'm sorry; I'm sorry for what has happened." He was so gracious. He just said "Let's not talk about the past. Let's talk about the future."'

Wilhelm Verwoerd recognizes, as so many do, that the road ahead will be very hard, but that every individual has a part to play: 'We should be committed to *all* the people in this country . . . It's a drop in the bucket, I know, but a drop I can take responsibility for . . . at a human level I can help to try to reconstruct a society dehumanized and broken in the name of good intentions.'

There could hardly be a more powerful sign of reconciliation in South Africa. Those who care for that, and I hope that is everyone, might take the earliest opportunity to give money to Christian Aid or the Anti-apartheid Movement or the Church of Scotland for rebuilding in South Africa.

The last thing we could perhaps all agree on is Jesus Christ, the good shepherd. That shepherding theme lies behind all our Scripture readings this morning; it lies behind most of our hymns. We do the good shepherd theme less than justice, however, if we think of it merely in terms of our own salvation. However much it means to think of yourself as the wandering sheep whom the good shepherd will rescue, the Bible's theme is more than that. For the Bible it is a whole flock, a people, the whole nation, whom God will shepherd. 'The Lord of hosts will care for his people . . . I shall whistle to call them in, for I have delivered them', says the book of Zechariah. The future of South Africa must not be left simply in the hands of politicians and teachers and miners and soldiers and journalists. It must be committed to the great shepherd of the sheep whose name is praised throughout that land, in all communities of different backgrounds, with a fervour we know little of in Edinburgh.

Cry, the Beloved Country ends with Rev. Stephen Kumalo, the pastor, the shepherd of his people, at prayer.

He rose to his feet, and took off his hat and laid it down on the earth, and clasped his hands before him. And while he stood there the sun rose in the east. Yes, it is the dawn that has come . . . The sun tips with light the mountains of Angeli and East Griqualand . . . For it is the dawn that has come, as it has come for a thousand centuries, never

139

failing. But when *that* dawn will come, of our emancipation from the fear of bondage and the bondage of fear, why, that is a secret.

Pray for South Africa.
Let us pray:
God bless Africa; guard her peoples, guide her leaders; give her peace. Amen.

AFTER DUNBLANE

(After half a class of five-year-old schoolchildren and
their teacher were murdered and the rest of the class
horribly injured)

Dearly beloved, what shall we do with our grief?

Let us learn how to come together and be full of woe. Let
us learn from the Bible, from these terrible words of
Lamentations we read this morning: 'For these things I
weep: my eyes flow with tears; for a comforter is far from
me, one to revive my courage; my children are desolate, for
the enemy has prevailed.'

Let us learn from great literature: from the achievements of
ancient Greece, a whole culture of art based on public
expressions of lament. Or from Shakespeare, whose tragedies
unlock in us the deepest pain in ourselves and in the human
situation.

One of the real benefits of counselling in my lifetime has
been to help us all to understand that to mourn and grieve
is good and right and human. I would not go so far as to
say that it is unhealthy for people to show relatively little
emotion as they adjust to grief; sometimes individuals can
be made to feel guilty for not grieving enough. We are all
different and it is not true that people who prefer not to talk
about feelings are likely to be suffering from impacted grief
and be unhealthy in the long run.

But I do believe that we need to deal with grief. One of
the books which helped me understand what that might
mean is Jean Morrison's book called *Loss*. We need to deal
with grief, in different ways for different people. For some,
talking about their feelings is the only way; but for all, we
need to mourn. It is certainly true that to ignore grief or to

postpone it or to feel ashamed of it is damaging and unhealthy; and we need to discover what to do with our grief. Both inside each one of us. I guarantee that you have been aware this week of deep feelings inside yourself that you did not know, or had forgotten, were there. And also together, in public. I knew there would be more people than usual in church today. To have a time of silence together, to lament, to share our grief.

Dearly beloved, what shall we do with our belonging together?

To say that we have all been 'caught up together' in the unspeakable moment of Wednesday morning is to be platitudinous: but it is also to say something very important. For we have glimpsed this week something that Christian faith has tried to say from the very first, but which we find so difficult to hear. Namely, that we do all belong together. We are part of Dunblane and Dunblane is part of us.

The shared sorrow has united the nation. I suspect we were all grateful to politicians this week. George Robertson and Michael Forsyth holding each other up, the House of Commons as no one has seen it before, and on Friday, so good, John Major and Tony Blair going together. The shared sorrow has united the nation.

> No man is an island, entire of itself. . . . Any man's death diminishes me, because I am involved with mankind. And therefore never send to know for whom the bell tolls; it tolls for thee. (Donne)

We have glimpsed this week our common humanity: that we are united by being members of the human race and that that matters more than the differences of temperament and politics and religion and history which always divide us. After this week I know that those who say we are all merely individuals are lying or do not understand. For I know that we belong together and that those in Dunblane are our brothers and sisters. So can we not remember that, and build on that, and believe that, and live that? Live the conviction that those who suffer in London and New York and

142

Jerusalem and Cambodia are our brothers and sisters? Live the conviction that those who disagree with us are not our enemies but our fellow human beings? That those we don't like are not to be hated or feared or demonized, for they are our fellow human beings and we are part, indissolubly part, of common human life together?

Dearly beloved, what shall we do with our lives?

Never was there a more terrible demonstration of the fragility of human life. One moment, waving goodbye, and then never again. One moment setting out the gym for games, the next moment a mediaeval painting of hell. One moment just another Wednesday morning, the next moment Dunblane the worst place in the world. How insubstantial is the thread that holds us to life. The Bible is right: 'all flesh is grass.' Tennyson is right:

> Man comes and tills the field and lies beneath,
> And after many a summer dies the swan.

Oh the pity of it that we waste so much of these brief lives of ours on the things that do no good! That so much of our time we spend running after the things that do not matter; that so much of our time we spend on needless efforts and endeavours; that so much of our time we spend on silly argument; that so much of our time we spend in the most second-rate parts of ourselves!

What shall we do with our lives? Anyone who has been rescued from death will tell you that they have a strong sense of mortality and a real determination to use the rest of their lives to do some good. And they will tell you that that sense fades over the years as they return to the same kind of lives they lived before. This week, conscious of the fragile hold we have on this earth, what shall we do with our lives? I have mentioned before the saying of the old monks to those who were learning how to be Christians: 'If you knew that you would die tomorrow, what would you do today? Now, go and do it.'

Dearly beloved, what shall we do with our religion?

Shall we try to worship and love a terrible being who plans

143

the destruction of five-year-olds? Shall we say, as many people said after Aberfan and as the journalist Polly Toynbee said on the radio on Thursday, 'For me this is the final clarification that there is no God, or if there is that God is one I want nothing to do with'? Shall we take refuge in theology and persuade ourselves that it is all to do with free will and the irrational nature of evil and the doctrine of the Fall and professors of theology must be able to understand it so there is bound to be an answer somewhere?

Or shall we rage and weep and lament before God? Rage and weep and lament and pray. As so much of the Bible does. Rage and weep and lament and pray with God. Shall we commit ourselves to the God who meets us in the un-limited, unutterable love of Jesus Christ and his cross: and trust that somehow he is the very heart of how things are? That his weakness and suffering and love which never stops children from dying or parents grieving or a town having its heart ripped out is still real and central and will somehow start to heal the accursed horror of Dunblane. That evil, however dreadful, however powerful, may not be able to have the last word. That the God of Jesus Christ is the one I will hold to however hard it is and whenever it is hardest.

To say that may be as much as it is right and possible for Christians to say at this moment. Many will call it useless, and I can understand that. But for others, and for me, it may be the only thing which makes this week bearable. Who could trust anyone who tried to explain this week? You could only have confidence in a kind of religion which spoke of darkness and mystery and depth; and of life and love and light shining in the darkness so that the darkness could not put it out.

Rabbi Hugo Gryn heard this story from his uncle who was there. In Buchenwald concentration camp there was a group of particularly learned Jews, several of them rabbis. One Sunday afternoon in their despair, they took up the idea of putting God on trial. So witnesses came forward for the prose-cution, others for the defence, and a bench of rabbis acted as judges. The case for the prosecution was overwhelming.

144

Their community was being wiped out; most of their families had already been destroyed; how could a good God permit this to happen? The case having been made and a desperate defence put up, the judges had little difficulty in reaching their verdict: the accused was guilty as charged, guilty of neglecting his people. Silence fell upon the court, until one elderly inmate rose to his feet. 'Nevertheless', he said, 'Let us not forget. It is time for our evening prayers.'

Amen.